Hosea

Michael A. Eaton

Christian Focus

By the same author

1, 2, 3 John (Christian Focus)
Ecclesiastes (Tyndale Commentary, IVP)
The Baptism with the Spirit (IVP)
How To Live A Godly Life (Sovereign World)
Walk in the Spirit (Word)
Living Under Grace (Romans 6-7) (Nelson Word)
How To Enjoy God's Worldwide Church (Sovereign World)
Theology of Encouragement (Paternoster)
Preaching Through the Bible: 1 Samuel (Sovereign World)

© Michael A. Eaton
ISBN 1 85792 277 8
Published in 1996 by Christian Focus Publications, Geanies House,
Fearn, Ross-shire, IV20 1TW, Great Britain.
Cover design by Donna Macleod

Contents

Preface

Like other published expositions of mine, on 1 Samuel and 1-3 John, these pages are a by-product of my preaching. In preaching my design is not so much to impart information as to change lives! I never try to teach 'pure' doctrine or 'pure' bible-study. Although I am sometimes called an 'expository preacher' I am pleased if the emphasis is more on the word 'preacher' than on the word 'expository'. I am wanting to make sure that the people to whom I preach are never the same again. It is an ideal which is not always reached!

'Hosea' is a book that I have been slow to preach on because the Hebrew text is rugged, and the structure of the book is difficult to discern. I first tried my hand at speaking on it in a midweek prayer meeting of Lusaka Baptist Church, a long time ago. I would expound a few verses for a few minutes each week before the fellowship turned to prayer which was the main concern of the evening. But recently I have felt a little more ready for the challenge of Hosea. The lunchtime meetings at City Hall, Nairobi, have heard some of it. Chrisco Central Church, Nairobi, heard some more. The preacher's style of putting one's material across in a small number of points is still visible in this material and I have been happy to leave it this way in the hope that it might help those whose work it is to expound and apply the Word of God. In the actual delivery of these 'messages' I let myself wander far and wide, and gave myself to pressing their relevance upon the people in a manner that was often more extemporary than expository! Nevertheless the 'kernel' of such messages was an interpretation of the message of Hosea. If some of the preaching comes through in this version, so much the better! Each expositor has to have his own interests and his own approach. My exposition sets out the material in the kind of points a preacher might have in his notes.

There are some good commentaries on Hosea. Seventeen of them are mentioned in my footnotes, to which might be added that of E.B. Pusey (*The Minor Prophets*) of which I used the beautiful

7

folio edition of 1860. Works by T. Laetsch (*The Minor Prophets*, Concordia, 1956), E. Jacob (Osee, Delachaux & Niestle, 1965) and J. Jeremias (*Der Prophet Hosea*, Vandenhoeck & Ruprecht, 1983), plus the special studies by H.S. Nyberg (*Studien zum Hoseabuch*, Uppsala Universitets Arsskrift, 1935) and W. Kuhnigk (*Nordwestsemitische Studien zum Hoseabuch*, Pontifical Biblical Institute, 1974) are also outstanding in different ways. My personal favourite is F.I. Andersen and D.N. Freedman's superb volume (*Hosea*, Anchor Bible, Doubleday, 1980) which, with all its intricacies and technicalities, is stimulating and often provocative. The exposition of Hosea 14 by the Puritan Richard Sibbes (*The Returning Backslider*) is exegetically weak but interesting and useful in its own way.

However, my purpose in preaching and writing this material was not to give the substance one might find in these excellent works, many of them deliciously fat and juicy, but to turn the written word into the 'prophetic' word. My chapters here can each be read in less than ten minutes. But the original sermons took much longer, sometimes 60 minutes or so. Sometimes a random remark, which might have nothing to do with Hosea, was the very remark which pierced someone's heart. 'Eagerly desire spiritual gifts', said Paul, 'especially the gift of prophecy' (1 Corinthians 14:1). What I have wanted more than anything else is for 'teaching' to become 'prophecy'.

So I have not side-stepped the study of Hosea, but the detailed study is under the surface rather than floating on top. What is 'floating on the top' is an attempt to apply the message of Hosea to my own life and the lives of others.

For chronological matters, I have followed Thiele's *Mysterious Numbers of the Hebrew Kings* (Paternoster, 1965), with a few improvements (see L. McFall, Has the chronology of the Hebrew kings been finally settled? in *Themelios*, 17:1 (Oct/Nov 1991), pp. 6-11).

I have provided my own translation of Hosea which has fewer textual emendations than in many commentaries. And I have tried to present the message of each section rather than the minutiae of exegetical disputes, although the task of exegesis has not been omitted. I have wanted to provide a line of theological exposition without too many distractions. Nor have I wanted to clutter up the text with explanations of Hebrew grammar, yet, occasionally, this is unavoidable.

I am again grateful to friends who have been a stimulus and encouragement to me, especially the people of Chrisco Fellowship, Nairobi, Kenya, where my material generally gets its first hearing. I am grateful for the encouragements of my family, especially to my daughter Mrs Kyrstina Gysling who reduces the number of slips in my work, and to Christian Focus publishers who asked for my work on 1-3 John and on Hosea.

Michael Eaton,
Nairobi

CHIEF ABBREVIATIONS

ASV: Bible, American Standard Version, 1901.
AV: Bible, Authorised Version (1611)
GNB: Good News Bible: Today's English Version (1976 ed).
JB: Jerusalem Bible
MT: Massoretic Text
NAB: New American Bible
NASB: Bible, New American Standard Version
NCV: Bible, New Century Version
NEB: New English Bible
NIV: Bible, New International Version
REB: Revised English Bible
RSV: Bible, Revised Standard Version
RV: Bible, Revised Version

INTRODUCTION

Every preacher finds that his background influences the way he preaches. For example, Isaiah's call to ministry began with a gripping vision of the holiness of God. It permeated his teaching for the rest of his life. Paul began his life as a Christian with a meeting with Jesus Christ in his resurrection glory. It was that vision that gave rise to Paul's entire convictions about Jesus, about salvation and about ministry.

Hosea's transforming experience was not a vision of the holiness of God, nor a meeting with the risen Jesus. It was a difficult marriage! God overruled in Hosea's life to bring him through a very painful experience. His intense sufferings in a marriage which was difficult from the beginning, and for some years was entirely ruptured, brought him to know the love of God as never before. If in the New Testament John is the 'apostle of love', in the Old Testament Hosea is the prophet of love.

Hosea and His Times
Israel commenced as a nation when it was 'redeemed by the blood of the lamb'. Its leaders were Moses, Joshua and then various judges, until the time when the people demanded a king. The first king, Saul, was a failure. God's model king was David (1010-970 BC), who handed over a powerful kingdom to his son Solomon (970-930), and for a few years there was a golden age of prosperity and international influence for Israel. But towards the end of Solomon's reign he introduced idolatry, and when he died the nation split into two, northern Israel (often called 'Ephraim' after its largest tribe), and Judah in the south. It is mainly the northern part of the country that is the concern of the book of Hosea.

The northern kingdom of Israel lasted for over 200 years, from 930 to 723. Hosea ministered in its last days (755 to 723). This 200-year history can be divided into four sections.

First there were *the years under Jeroboam I and his successors.* Jeroboam started an idolatrous tradition in Israel. The reasons were political. He wanted to establish the northern kingdom as a separate kingdom from Judah, and so he did not want his people to be visiting the temple in Jerusalem. He invented his own idols to persuade the people to worship in his newly made sanctuaries in Dan and Bethel. His new religion was idolatrous and 'made Israel to sin'. The nation never recovered from what he did. The following five kings (Nadab, Baasha, Elah, Zimri, Tibni) brought no changes. The idolatry of Jeroboam I continued.

A second phase in the story of northern Israel came with *the dynasty of Omri.* Omri became king in 880 after five years of civil war. He introduced an even more serious paganism into Israel. His son Ahab made Baal-worship the state-religion of northern Israel and the worship of the LORD became an underground movement for many years. Elijah and Elisha held much of the country to its old ways, but the paganism of Ahab and his wife Jezebel continued. Their children Ahaziah and Joram ruled for a while, but then the line came to an end.

A third phase in the story came with *Jehu.* He was commissioned by God to remove Ahab's regime from Israel. He did so with great cruelty and then sponsored his own form of idolatry. Jehu's son and grandson ruled after him. Then came Jehu's great-grandson, Jeroboam II. After Jeroboam came his son, Zechariah who was murdered and the line came to an end. Hosea's ministry began at this time, in the reign of Jeroboam II.

The fourth phase in the story is *the time when the country had six kings in thirty years.* Shallum murdered Zechariah (753), the last of the line of Jeroboam, Shallum reigned for one month and was himself murdered by Menahem (752). Menahem passed the throne to his son Pekahiah (742). Pekahiah was murdered by Pekah (740). In due course Pekah was murdered by Hoshea (not Hosea the prophet!) in 732/1 and the kingdom came to an end altogether in 723. This stage of Israel's history consisted of thirty years of political assassinations and intrigues of one kind or another.

In the days of Jeroboam II Israel became prosperous. These
were days of economic stability; the nation was affluent. However, after the death of Jeroboam II, the nation was characterised
by much political strife both internally and in its international rela-
tions. Israel was tempted to turn to Assyria for help (see 5:13; 8:9),
but Egypt was also thought to be a possible refuge in time of trouble. After Jeroboam died, there were the six kings mentioned above
and then the nation ceased to exist. The nation had constantly sought
human expedients and had refused to amend its idolatrous and unjust ways (see 7:3, 16; 8:4; 2 Kings chapters 15-18).

Hosea ministered throughout this fourth stage of Israel's history.
The shortest possible length of his ministry, given the data in Hosea
1:1, is the 23-year period from 752 (Jeroboam II's last year) to 729
(Hezekiah's first year as co-regent). It is probable that the ministry
of Hosea was longer than this, say from 760-723. It would be strange
to say that the Word of the Lord came to Hosea in the days of
Jeroboam if there had not been at least a few years during Jeroboam's reign when Hosea ministered, and there are parts of the book
of Hosea that certainly date from the days of Jeroboam. So we may
reckon that Hosea's ministry lasted from about 760 to 723, a period
of 37 years. His ministry in northern Israel would have been brought
to an end by the time of the fall of Samaria (723). He may have
continued in retirement in Judah after this date, but we have no
prophetic oracles from that time, and for the purpose of studying
his prophecy, the ministry of Hosea may be regarded as running
from 760 to 723.

At different times in the story of Israel, the nation had different
enemies. When Israel first invaded Canaan the main enemy was
the Philistines. The days of Solomon were relatively peaceful, but
as the power of the northern kingdom deteriorated the Arameans
(or Syrians) became the nation's main enemy. Jeroboam II was
able to resist the power of the Arameans, but after he died, the
Arameans and Israelites became allies and tried to invade Judah.
Judah foolishly, as we shall see, appealed to Assyria for help and
in 732 the Arameans were defeated. After 732 the main enemy for

Israel and Judah were the Assyrians, and it was they who destroyed Samaria in 723 and brought the northern kingdom of Israel to an end.

Hosea bears witness to a very decadent society in the last half-century of the nation's existence. Loose living abounded. We read of drunkenness (7:3-7), armed robbery, adultery, murder. The leadership of the nation was corrupt (4:1-2; 5:1-2; 6:6, 9; 7:1, 6-7). The underlying cause of all of this was corrupt religion. People worshipped the 'Baals'. The word 'baal' means 'lord'. 'Baal' (who had various manifestations so that the plural, Baals or Baalim, can also be used) was the fertility god of the Canaanites. He was thought to have control over wind, rain and clouds, and so over fertility. In the days of Ahab, Jezebel had built a temple for Baal (1 Kings 16:31b-32) and had made an 'Asherah-pole', an upright statue designed to represent a goddess of fertility (1 Kings 16:33). The law demanded that such idols be cut down (Exodus 23:34) or burned (Deuteronomy 12:3).

Despite the savage extermination of one form of idolatry by Jehu, the various fertility cults had come back into Israel in Hosea's days. The people were indulging in immoral 'worship' on the tops of hills (4:13) and had centres of worship at Bethel and Gilgal (9:15; 12:11). They used various images (8:5; 13:2; 14:8), including golden calves, and had idolatrous altars (8:11; 12:11), incense (11:2; 4:13), and sacred pillars (10:1-2). They consulted spirits (4:12). The worship played into the lascivious inclinations of men and women, and also seemed to offer a God-given success in agricultural affairs (4:13-14). Hosea says that the entire facade must be destroyed (3:4; 9:1). This worship seems to have been addressed to 'Yahweh', but the true God of Israel, the true Yahweh, did not want it (2:16). The people must turn to God (6:1-6), said Hosea, and live in mercy and righteousness (6:6). But they will never do so voluntarily. They will be chastised and then there will be a way of their returning and finding salvation (2:16; 3:5; chapter 14).

14 HOSEAHOSEA

Hosea and His Family

We may guess that Hosea was born about 785. His father's name was Beeri. Hosea was a young man, loyal to the faith of the house of David in the south, and aged in his middle twenties (we might guess) when he was called to be a prophet. His prophetic call was at one and the same time a call to get married. However, the marriage of Hosea is a matter of some dispute.

As described in Hosea chapter 1, Hosea's marriage has been taken in at least the following four ways.

(i) There was a time when Hosea 1:2 was widely taken to refer to a vision or a parable rather than an actual event.

(ii) Others have assumed that *every* girl in northern Israel was guilty of immorality because of the pagan religion of the land. Hosea was simply marrying a typical north Israelite girl.

(iii) Others understand it to mean that Hosea was called to marry a 'cult prostitute', a temple-prostitute who had been involved in the immoralities of the pagan rites of north Israel.

(iv) Another view is that Hosea took a woman whom he thought would be pure only to find out *later* that she was immoral. Hosea, then, discovered the purpose of God in what had happened to him. On this view 'woman of harlotry' either means 'woman with immoral tendencies', or the narrative is projecting into the past what only became obvious later.

Some of these interpretations seem to arise from a desire to save the good names of Hosea and Gomer. My own view (which agrees with that of McComiskey)[1] is that Hosea was commanded to marry an immoral girl, who had already some children as the result of her immoralities. This seems to be the most straightforward reading of the text.

There are several guidelines in interpretation.

(i) The words cannot naturally be taken to refer to a parable or to a vision. They clearly point to an actual experience in Hosea's lifetime.

---

1. T.E. McComiskey, Hosea, in *The Minor Prophets*, vol. 1 (McComiskey and others, Baker, 1992), pp. 11-17.

(ii) The phrase 'take to yourself a woman of harlotry and children of harlotry...' must be interpreted carefully. 'Take' on its own could refer to an illicit relationship but 'Take ... a woman' is the normal way of speaking of marriage, and 'Take a child' can refer to adoption (see Esther 2:7). The genitive phrase '... of harlotry' must have adjectival force: 'a woman characterised by her present immorality'. It cannot naturally be made to mean a woman who *will* be promiscuous at some future date. Also, Hosea is to take 'Children of harlotry', children born as the result of adultery. The Hebrew implies that the taking of the wife and the taking of the children occur at the same time. ('Take' is one verb with two objects.)

All of this seems to imply that Hosea was asked to marry a woman who was immoral, and already had children as the result of her immoralities. The prophets could be asked to do strange things at times. Isaiah walked the streets of Jerusalem naked and barefoot (Isaiah 20:2). Ezekiel cooked a meal with dung (Ezekiel 4:12). What Hosea 1:2 says is that God commanded Hosea to marry an immoral woman. Although it was illegal for a priest to do such a thing it was not against the Mosaic law for any others.

This interpretation also fits the precise situation in Israel. It was not the case that Israel was pure at first and then fell into spiritual adultery. Rather Israel was guilty of spiritual unfaithfulness from the very earliest days. Statements about Israel's good beginnings do not actually speak of her *purity;* Israel responded well to God but was full of idolatrous inclinations.

(iii) There is not much biographical detail to satisfy our curiosity but as best as we can see the story is as follows. At some time in the reign of Jeroboam II, maybe about 760, and maybe when he was about twenty-five years old, Hosea met and fell in love with a girl named Gomer who was known for her immoral ways, and had several children already. His call to be a prophet came at this time and at God's instruction he married Gomer and adopted her children. They then began to have children of their own. Later his wife fell back into her old ways and she deserted Hosea.

A similar story comes in chapter 3. Some think it is the same story told again, an almost duplicate version of chapter 1. Others think it is the story of a different woman, and that Hosea himself had some polygamous tendencies! The most natural understanding is that it again refers to Gomer but that the occasion is a later one. Gomer fell into slavery, and God called Hosea to go to the rescue of his estranged wife. Hosea did as he was instructed, bought his wife out of slavery, insisted on a lengthy period of deprivation, and then took her back. Nothing more is told us, but the story only makes sense on the assumption that from that point on they lived together happily!

(iv) The entire experience was obviously exceedingly painful but it was so closely analogous to the relationship between God and Israel that the events of Hosea's life, though they actually happened, were virtually a parable of the spiritual relationship between God and his people. God chose a bride. She was impure from the very earliest days, but responded in faith and was in a good relationship to God for a generation or so. Then the nation fell into sin, and subsequently into bondage. God lets his people fall into serious calamities and distresses as Gomer had fallen into slavery. But the time will come when God will redeem his people and after disciplining them will resume a marriage relationship with them. The pain that the soft and tender-hearted Hosea had experienced expressed God's love and desire for his people. 'How can I give you up?' was the cry of Hosea. 'How can I give you up?' was the cry of God.

Hosea and His Book

At some stage towards the end of Hosea's ministry, or perhaps in retirement years in Judah, a resumé of some of Hosea's prophecy was written up and the document we have was produced.

There are three aspects to it that are of importance to us: (i) its text and translation, (ii) its integrity as a unified book, and (iii) its structure.

(i) Firstly, let us consider its text. The original documents of the Old Testament were written in a Hebrew script that had no vowels. Vowels were used in speaking, obviously, but not at first in written Hebrew. As copies of the original were made it could happen that tiny textual variations would arise in the Hebrew manuscripts. As the manuscripts were recopied variations among the manuscripts crept in. An 'R' could look like a 'D'. The Hebrew for 'witnesses' (with a Hebrew D) looked like the Hebrew for 'cities' (with a Hebrew R; see Isaiah 33:8 NIV). A phrase could slip out (see Genesis 4:8 NIV). Or a phrase could be wrongly inserted (see the Dead Sea Scroll of Isaiah 53:11; note NIV). These variations concern only tiny matters of detail.

The work of 'textual criticism' compares manuscripts so as to get back to the original. There is plenty of evidence that the standard text which Old Testament scholars use is highly trustworthy. For much of the time, and for all practical purposes, the ordinary Christian need not bother about textual variants so long as a reliable translation is being used. The NASB and NIV may be recommended. Hosea is a difficult text in this respect and we shall have to give the matter some attention.

From about the 7th to 9th centuries AD Hebrew-speaking rabbis placed vowels into the Hebrew text of the Old Testament. The 'un-pointed' Hebrew text (that is, without vowels) is not difficult to read if the language is *thoroughly* known. Jewish 'Massoretes', ('transmitters') went to incredible lengths to preserve the accuracy of the copying. They could read an unpointed text easily, just as an Israeli teenager can read an unpointed Hebrew newspaper today. The Massoretes invented systems of 'pointing' to represent vowel sounds. Two particular Jewish families, the Ben Asher family and the Ben Naphtali family were famous for this work. The modern Old Testament scholar does his work on the 'Massoretic Text' (the MT) which consists of the original text to which Massoretic pointing has been added. It used to be thought that the vowel-points were as original as the consonants. However this was a mistake. They began to be introduced in the 6th or 7th centuries AD.

Because the Hebrew text of Hosea is more difficult than most parts of the Old Testament, Old Testament scholars have tended in the past to 'emend' the Hebrew text of Hosea excessively. When the text is difficult they have often held the view that the Hebrew needs improving. They often consult ancient translations and translate back into Hebrew. The Old Testament was, in pre-Christian times, translated into two major ancient languages. After the fourth century BC, Jews outside of Israel began to speak Greek, so that from the third century onwards Greek translations of the Old Testament became available. In Israel people began to speak Aramaic, and needed an Aramaic paraphrase of the Hebrew text. These 'targums' ['paraphrases'] were initially only oral but later they were written down. These translations and some later ones, including those in Latin and in Syriac, are used to get back to the original.

Some of this work has been done in an unsatisfactory manner. It often happens that the Hebrew text has been reconstructed by intelligent guesswork. Ancient translations are not always reliable. Their translators appear to have done some intelligent guessing of their own. Sometimes to follow an ancient translation is no more than to follow ancient ignorance. This means that in the past 'textual criticism' has often been done in a very unsatisfactory way. In the New English Bible (NEB), for example, there are about 90 'emendations' in the book of Hosea, just under half of them based on ancient translations and just over half of them based on intelligent guesswork. But the methodology of Old Testament textual criticism as currently practised is often unsatisfactory. What Christian wants to be treating as the Word of God a translation from Hebrew of something that does not exist in any manuscript in the world but was invented by some scholar a few years ago? Textual criticism is a necessary task – there is no doubt about that – but it has to be done with better principles than have been followed in the last century or so. For this reason it is important to use Old Testament translations that do not follow speculations in their translation-work. One test of a good translation for a Christian who is looking at Scripture as God's Word is how it handles the Old Testament textual difficulties. Translations like the NEB, the Revised English Bible (REB), the New American Bible (NAB, a Roman Catholic work not to be confused with the New American Standard Bible), the Jerusalem Bible (JB), the Good News Bible (GNB), and others have a high quantity of 'emendations'. Often the scholar *writes* his own Hebrew text before he translates it! One needs to be on surer ground than this. The consonantal Hebrew text passed down by the 'Massoretes' has signs of great accuracy. It should only be emended in its consonantal readings where there is very substantial reasons for doing so. Even the vowel-pointing of the MT is surprisingly reliable and should not be lightly emended.

The most reliable handy translations for detailed study of the Bible are the New International Version (NIV) and the New American Standard Bible (NASB). Also the English Revised Version (RV) of 1881 and 1885 was a very accurate translation, especially in its American version known as the American Standard Version (1901). Since the 1960s about a dozen translations have been competing for popularity. The NASB is very accurate but does not read well in public. The NIV reads well, but it breaks away from the Authorised Version (AV) tradition in a way that gives it a slightly 'foreign' atmosphere in Christian circles dominated by the AV. If the accuracy of the NASB could be combined with greater literary sensitivity we would have a near-perfect English Bible. At the moment English-speaking Christians have the NIV and the NASB as the two best modern translations for detailed study.

All of this is preliminary to saying that in the translation provided in the pages below I have kept close to the Massoretic Text and have translated it in a way that is close to the AV, RV, Revised Standard Version (RSV), NIV and NASB styles of translating. In the following exposition I have not emended the consonantal text except at one point where there is definite evidence that it is required (at 7:14). There are more places where I have felt the vowel-pointing or division of words could be profitably read in another way (in 1:4; 4:4, 7, 11-12, 14; 5:13; 6:5; 7:4; 8:2; 10:6, 11; 11:2, 5,

7). Details are given at the appropriate points in the exposition. One must remember that the vowel-pointing is not original but stems from, at least, the 9th century AD.

Nowadays more is known of Semitic languages and some difficulties in the Hebrew text have received explanation that was not available at the time of pre-twentieth century translations. Scholars are nowadays less happy with slapdash and indiscriminate emendations. It is notable that the commentary on Hosea by the highly qualified Hebraist and linguist, F.I. Andersen, emends the consonants only rarely and reluctantly. My procedure is the same. This is a much more satisfactory procedure than excessive and unrestrained emendations.

(ii) The next matter that requires consideration is the question as to whether Hosea has been given a 'Judean redaction'. There are fourteen references to Judah and one to 'David' in Hosea (1:7, 11; 3:5; 4:15; 5:5, 10, 12, 13, 14; 6:4, 10-11; 8:14; 10:11; 11:12 and 12:2). Sometimes it is thought that some of these were inserted into the document at a later stage and are not original. Wolff thought 1:7 is 'secondary' and that 'David their king' is a later addition in 3:5, as also are (thought Wolff) the words 'and Judah' in 4:15, and the line 'Judah also stumbles with them' in 5:5, and the mention of Judah in 6:11. He thought that 'Judah' should read 'Israel' in 12:2.[2] G.I. Davies thinks the majority of references to Judah are later insertions.[3]

However there is no good reason for this procedure. Some of the references to Judah are indisputably original because they form part of the poetic structure of the text, and cannot be deleted without damaging that structure. But if some references are indisputably original, no objective reasons exist for deleting the others which are similar to them.

---

2. H.W. Wolff, *Hosea* (Hermeneia, Fortress, 1974), pp. 9, 57, 72, 95, 106, 206.

3. G.I. Davies, *Hosea* (Old Testament Guides, JSOT, 1993), p. 13.

It ought to be noticed also that Hosea 1:7 probably should have a different translation from the one that is common. Most translations of 1:7 have something like 'I will not yet again pity the house of Israel ... Yet I will show love to the house of Judah...'. This draws a contrast between Israel and Judah. Taken this way commentators have often noted that it is out of harmony with Hosea's message. Many commentators wish to delete it or think the text is corrupt and the word 'not' has been omitted from the text. The difficulties are overcome if it is realised that the phrase 'not yet again' extends over four verbs, and the Hebrew preposition *b* (often translated 'by') may mean 'from' with verbs of departure or verbs of rescue.

The Hebrew may be over-literally translated: '...Call her name Lo-Ruhammah for I will not *yet again pity* the house of Israel, for I will surely [*not yet again*] forgive them. [7]And the house of Judah I will [*not yet again*] pity, and I will [*not yet again*] save them as Yahweh their God. And I will not save them from the bow or from the sword or from war, from horses or horsemen.'

It will be noted that the phrase 'not yet again' continues to have force four times with the verbs 'pity', 'forgive', 'pity' and 'save'. Most translations sense that the negative force has to extend over two verbs. REB has 'I shall never again show love ... never again forgive...', but the 'never again' may continue over the next two verbs also.

It is also important to notice that with verbs indicating 'motion away' the following Hebrew preposition *b* has the sense of 'from'. (It is not that *b* on its own means 'from', but that it has the English sense of 'from' with verbs indicating some kind of departure. The 'from-ness' is in the verb not in the preposition, but in English it means that *b* is best translated as 'from'.)

Recent studies of Hebrew have shown occasions in the Hebrew Bible where the force of a particle or preposition continues over several phrases. It can do 'double duty' or 'multiple duty'. We find this also in English. We might say 'I will not come and see you'. The 'not' is doing 'double duty'. It means 'I will not come and I will not see you'. The same phenomenon is found in Hebrew.

This makes much better sense. Nowhere in Hosea does God treat Israel one way and Judah another way. On the contrary! 'The Israelites stumble ... Judah also stumbles with them' (5:5). God is a lion to Israel, and a lion to Judah alike (5:14) and asks 'What can I do?' about both nations equally (6:4). The customary translation of 1:7 contradicts those places where Israel and Judah are treated in totally parallel manner (see also 5:12,13; 6:10-11; 8:14; 10:11). Both Judah and Israel can be restored, but both of them are to be restored 'in the latter days' after thorough abandonment and chastening. Both Judah and Israel are in effect to be 'resurrected' after the death of their covenant-relationship with God. The message of Hosea is not that God will chasten Israel but not Judah. Rather it is that God will chasten Israel and Judah to the point of death and abandonment, but then will raise his people when a second David comes to rescue them.

Judah was the location of the promises of God. There were no promises to Samaria comparable to those given to Jerusalem. 'Salvation is of the Jews', said Jesus (John 4:22), and his words reflected hundreds of years of history. The hope of God's people revolved around something God would do in Jerusalem. After the division of the kingdom in 931/930, despite what had happened, the hope of Israel continued to be in the south. Even a northern prophet would think this way if he were a true prophet at all. The Messiah would be a second 'David' (Hosea 3:5). Hosea's book had to have a Judean viewpoint if it was to be true to God's promises of salvation. Hosea lived in the north but he could not totally neglect the fact that God's purpose was for the whole of Israel and that his promises centred in what he would do in Jerusalem. The title to the book (1:1) has a Judean viewpoint; it lists Judah's kings more than those of Israel. Hosea may or may not have been responsible for the title, but it certainly reflects the standpoint of his preaching. The Judean references simply mean that although Hosea's ministry was located in the northern kingdom he had to take Judah into account also.

(iii) A third aspect of the book of Hosea requiring consideration is the discernment of its arrangement. Most books of the Bible are well edited, some of them brilliantly. J.A. Motyer, for example, has shown that Isaiah is skilfully edited and is a literary masterpiece.[4] Some books which have been thought to be poorly edited probably have more structure than has been acknowledged.[5] But in the case of Hosea, no one has yet found a satisfactory key to the analysis of the book. The Puritan devotional commentator, Matthew Henry, was perceptive in thinking it was 'like the book of Proverbs, without connexion'.[6] I prefer to lay out the material in a simple manner. It may be that one day a more subtle arrangement signalled by Hosea himself will be discovered. The first three chapters are straight forward, but chapters 4-14 are more difficult. It is worth mentioning that the enumeration of the verses in the common English translations sometimes differs from that in the Hebrew editions (and in certain other Bibles). The differences are as follows.

English	Hebrew
1:10-11	2:1-2
2:1-21	2:3-25
11:12	12:1
12:1-14	12:2-15
13:16	14:1
14:1-9	14:2-10

The English enumeration is used in this book.

---

4. See J.A. Motyer, *The Prophecy of Isaiah* (IVP, 1993).
5. See my remarks on Ecclesiastes (in M.A. Eaton, *Ecclesiastes*, IVP, 1983) and on 1 John (in M.A. Eaton, *1, 2, 3 John*, Christian Focus, 1995).
6. *Matthew Henry's Commentary*, vol. 4 (Revell, New York, n.d.), p.1117.

1

The Family-life of Hosea and Its Message
(1:1-3:5)

1. An Unhappy Marriage (1:1-5)

The church has to go through varied conditions in its pilgrimage
through this world. In Old Testament times there were days of
success and favour as, for example, under David. There were also
periods of persecution like that experienced when Ahab and
Jezebel were ruling. There were eras too when God's people were
tolerated by pagan powers though their liberties were curtailed, as
in the times of Ezra, Nehemiah and beyond.

In our own day, in one part of the world the church may be
flourishing numerically with crowded buildings, while in another
it might be despised and neglected or even persecuted. At one time
it may have great courage and integrity. At another it might be
compromised by worldly ways and be tamely submissive to worldly
rulers.

In Hosea's days the politics of northern Israel were murder-
ously violent and conspiratorial. The economy was deceptively
prosperous during the days of Jeroboam but dropped rapidly in
subsequent years. Israel's social concern was non-existent so far
as one can tell. At the root of the entire situation was corrupt,
immoral and idolatrous religion. Hosea's message had to relate to
the precise situation of his day. He does not simply give himself to
systematic exposition of the Mosaic law. Rather, soaked in the
truth of that law, he now presents his own message for the days in
which he lives.

1. *Each age needs God's spokesmen with their own distinctive
message*. We need men and women with a message from God
which they will boldly and courageously press upon the people of
God.

The book of Hosea begins with a title: **The word of Yahweh
that came to Hosea son of Beeri during the reigns of Uzziah,
Jotham, Ahaz and Hezekiah, kings of Judah, and during the
reign of Jeroboam son of Joash king of Israel** (1:1).

The five kings highlight the varied situations of Hosea's times.
Uzziah was famous for the easy, prosperous days in which he lived,

and for his formal, inherited religion, his negligence of God's ways, and his little achievement for God.

Jotham was famous for tinkering with small things while forgetting big things. The Assyrian threat was growing, but Jotham was refining the beauty of the temple (2 Kings 15:35-38), straining out a gnat but swallowing a camel.

Ahaz was an unbelieving man who failed to learn the lessons of history. He sank to as low a level as any king of Judah had ever sunk, when he gave his son in human sacrifice (2 Kings 16:2-3), and he turned to the immoral worship of northern Israel (2 Kings 16:4).

Hezekiah loved God, hated idols, and was willing to get involved in actually making progress with God and for God. He removed high places, and broke down the apparatus that had been used in pagan worship. He was willing to do things that had never been done before. 'He trusted in the LORD God of Israel!' (2 Kings 18:5).

Jeroboam was famous for a long, prosperous reign badly used. He continued the idolatry of the first Jeroboam (2 Kings 14:24). His days were days of crime, immorality and injustice. Sanctuaries were crowded with worshippers but gods of fertility were worshipped. Decades of stability (790s to 750s) would be followed by decades of instability (750s to 720s) and the end of the nation. At the death of Jeroboam II (753 BC) the nation had only thirty years to survive. God did not want the nation to be totally exterminated without warning (2 Kings 2:27) and gave them another generation to consider their ways. Jeroboam's military success, like his economic success, was apt to promote self-confidence and nationalistic self-congratulation.

These were the situations in which Hosea proclaimed a God-given message.

2. *God's spokesmen rebuke spiritual adultery.* The opening verse also mentions Hosea himself. His central message was to warn about spiritual adultery. He was a man who had learned by very

painful experience. His traumatic marriage was used in his life to get him to feel the burden of the spiritual unfaithfulness of Israel.

² When Yahweh began to speak through Hosea, Yahweh said to Hosea, 'Go, take to yourself a wife of harlotry and adopt children of harlotry, for the land is committing great harlotry and so is forsaking Yahweh' (1:2).

The most natural way to take these words (see my comments above, pp 12-13) is that Hosea's call to be a prophet came in connection with a call to marry an immoral woman who already had children as the result of her immoralities. It was a shocking command, but then the prophets were sometimes urged to do shocking things. It was not against the Mosaic law, although generally it would be exceedingly unwise. Marriage is the deepest union possible between two people. It is the most intensely personal relationship that there is. It involves feelings, emotions and, perhaps, resentments and jealousies. Everything about marriage is intensely intimate. It is even participation in each other's bodies. It is the joining together of interests and concerns. It is the producing together of children. It is loyalty. If a wife or husband says one word against the other in public, the other feels betrayed. It is extreme sensitivity.

What then is spiritual adultery? It is broken conversation. It is when God is no longer speaking to or listening to his people, and when his people are no longer listening or speaking to him. It is prayerlessness. It is broken loyalty. It is fractured and dissevered channels of fellowship. There is no pain like the pain of disloyalty within marriage, and in Hosea's day this was the way God felt about Israel. 'The land commits great harlotry and so is forsaking Yahweh.' The essential sin of Israel was spiritual unfaithfulness, 'forsaking the Lord' (1:2), disloyalty (9:1), forsaking the compassion of God and turning to violence. They turned to other 'lovers', the Canaanite gods (2:5), who were treated with affection. God's demands were left aside (4:1-3) and the people turned to robbery and banditry (7:1). The leadership was affected; prophets (4:5), priests (4:6, 9) and king were all content with wickedness (7:3).

There was drunkenness (4:11; 7:5), immorality (4:11; 7:4), idolatry (4:12). Then the people turned to Assyria for help (5:13; 8:9) and there was plotting (7:6) and assassinations (7:7). Israel mixed herself with the ways of the nations (7:8; 8:8; 11:5), including Egypt (11:11; 12:1) from which the nation had once been rescued. Beneath the chaos was ingrained prayerlessness (7:7) at a national level (7:10, 14) and slander of God (7:13). Hosea sums it all up in one idea: spiritual adultery.

Many things tend to corrupt the church. The people may start 'using' God to get their own ways. The first generation lives for God and his will. The second generation decides that respectability is a good thing for business, and starts to 'use' God to get on in life, while not being too distinctive in lifestyle. Within no time at all the church becomes powerless. Then a little further still down the road the church becomes idolatrous. It starts worshipping a 'god' which is a reconstructed version of the God of the Bible, but is no longer God at all. Or the church may be corrupted by the influence of devious national rulers. The world either flatters the church or persecutes or ignores it, but the world never helps the church.

So the church of Jesus Christ has to face many varied temptations and pressures. Success is as dangerous as persecution. In Hosea's day, politics were corrupt, society was unjust, and religion was idolatrous. So what does the church need in these varied situations? It needs prophets or their equivalent, men and women with a message from God boldly proclaimed.

3. *God's spokesmen warn that inherited ways of violence arouse God's reprisal.* God used Hosea to warn that the brutality of Israel's society was about to receive its retribution.

The days of Hosea were days of great ferocity. One murder followed speedily after another. The situation originated in the days of Jehu, who, about eighty years before, had been commissioned to remove the idolatry of the house of Ahab (see 1 Kings 19:17). But the way in which he fulfilled his call was hateful. Jehu (841-814/3

BC) was one of the most violent men of human history. He killed
first Jehoram of Israel, then Ahaziah of Judah, then Jezebel (2 Kings
9:30-37), then Ahab's sons (2 Kings 10:1-11), and the Judean family of Ahaziah (2 Kings 10:12-14). His zeal for bloodthirsty slaughter went beyond his commission from God.

This is the background to Hosea 1:3-5.

**³And so he went and took Gomer the daughter of Diblaim, and
she conceived and bore him a son. ⁴And Yahweh said to him, 'Call
his name Jezreel; for in a little while I will visit the blood of Jezreel
on the house of Jehu, and I will put an end to the rule⁷ of the
house of Israel. ⁵And it shall be that on that day I will break the
bow of Israel in the valley of Jezreel.**

Jehu's line which began in bloodshed ended likewise. Zechariah,
Jehu's great-great-grandson, was murdered and was the last of
Jehu's line. Then another regime began (2 Kings 15:8-12). The
murderer was Shallum, but he was killed within a month (15:13-
16). Menahem, his successor, came from another family. His line
lasted for one more reign (15:17-22). Pekahiah his son was the
last of his short dynasty (15:23-26). Pekah who assassinated
Pekahiah was from a ninth family among the kings of Israel. He
too was assassinated (15:27-31). Later Hoshea killed Pekah. In
Hoshea's reign, the Assyrians brought the northern kingdom of
Israel to an end. It was never to be revived. Hosea's second child
with Gomer was given a name which spoke of the retribution that
would soon fall on generations of violence.

'Jezreel' was the place where Jehu slaughtered the house of
Ahab, with frenzied brutality (see 2 Kings 9-10). God had allowed
Jehu his four generations as he had promised (2 Kings 10:30), but
now the hatred and violence which had been in Jehu's heart and
had characterised his dynasty would itself be avenged. Presumably
this oracle comes from a period before the death of Jeroboam II.
Soon Jeroboam's son would become king but would be slaughtered

---

7. A Hebrew shewa should be read beneath the third letter of the word *mmlkt*. It
is in the construct state, not the absolute state.

and the line would come to an end. Thirty years later northern
Israel lost its identity altogether.

Violence is easier to bring into a land than to eradicate. In many
parts of the world, today's children are trained in violence via TV
programmes, and learn to practise blasting people out of existence
in computer games. Meanwhile one picks up the newspaper and
reads about 'the lessons of Hiroshima', 'fire-bombing' in World
War II, the situation in an African country where half a million of
one of its tribes were butchered, the horrors of the first 41 months
of war in a part of Europe, and so on.

The name of Hosea's son gave warning of coming judgement
upon the brutality of Israel's society. Yet the point of the warning
was to give the opportunity for change. The Lord leaves the blunt
threat without further comment, but the very fact that the people
have been warned leaves open the possibility that they might fall
upon their knees and ask for mercy.

Questions for reflection

1. Should the church's message vary from age to age?

2. Is it good that our personal experience should affect our message?

3. How should Christians react to violence in modern society?

2. Like the Sand on the Seashore (1:6-2:1)
God's threat to withdraw the blessings of his relationship towards
his people (verses 6-9) is followed in 1:10-2:1 by predictions of
wonderful restoration.

First, we consider *God's warning.* The name of Hosea's second
child forewarns that God's compassion was about to be withheld.

**6 And she conceived again and bore a daughter, and he said to
him 'Call her name Lo-Ruhammah for I will not yet again pity**

> the house of Israel, for I will not again utterly forgive them; [7]
> and to the house of Judah I will not again show pity, nor will I
> save them again as Yahweh their God; I will not save them from
> the bow or from the sword or from war, from horses or from
> horsemen' (1:6-7; for the translation, see pp.17-22).

Hosea 1:8 brings us to the birth of Hosea's third child.

> [8] And she weaned Lo-Ruhammah, and she conceived and bore a
> son. [9] And he said, 'Call his name Lo-Ammi, for you are not my
> people and I am not "I-Am" for you.'

The third child also speaks of an end to God's blessings upon his
people. All three children (unlike the ones he adopted) are Hosea's
children. There is no need to think the omission of 'to him' (compare 1:3) means that two of the three children were illegitimate.
Hebrew style progressively abbreviates repetitive stories.

God was not willing for Israel to be built upon a foundation of
violence. In Hosea's day several generations of kings continued in
the violent ways of Jehu. God decides it is time for the dynasty to
be removed. 'I will break the bow – the sign of military capability
– of Israel', says God (1:5). Israel will shortly lose the war with
Assyria. Now God says he will not *again* show compassion to Israel (1:6) or to Judah (1:7). The name 'Lo-Ruhammah' means 'Not
Pitied'. As events turned out, God did not deliver Israel from the
Assyrians in 723 nor Judah (more than a century later) from the
Babylonians. The principle that applied to northern Israel – that
God will not tolerate persistent sin in his people – will eventually
apply to Judah in the south also. If faithless Israel is followed in
sinful ways by her treacherous sister Judah (see Jeremiah 3:10) the
same destiny will come upon both of them: the abolition of their
national independence.

The name of the third child, 'Lo-Ammi' (which has the meaning 'Not My People') makes a similar point. God threatens the
reversal of what happened at Sinai when he took a people to himself, and said to them 'If you will obey my voice and keep my

covenant, then you shall be my own special treasure' (Exodus 19:6).
Now, after centuries, it is clear that the nation is not keeping God's
Sinai-covenant. Why should the nation be his 'special treasure' any
longer?

A key point in these verses is the word 'again' (the force of
which continues from verse 6 in the Hebrew). God will not *again*
show compassion. Time and time again God had heard the cries of
his people when they brought trouble upon themselves by their
own sinfulness. But there may come a time when God says 'Enough
is enough' and then it is 'not possible to renew them *again* unto
repentance' (see Hebrews 6:6). Israel as a nation had reached this
point, and Judah would reach it a century later.

It is possible for a relationship with God to become 'dead', at
least for a time. When Hosea speaks of the relationship being restored
he envisages not only a healing (6:1) but also a resurrection from
the dead (6:2). For a while God's relationship with northern Israel
'died', and northern Israel became an Assyrian province. Similarly,
for a while, God's relationship with Judah 'died' and they were
banished from his presence in Babylon. Hosea's children were given
predictive names. The war with Assyria would be lost. God would
refuse to rescue them *this* time. Eventually to the *whole* nation,
Judah included, God would say, 'Right now, you are not my people.'

Second, we consider *God's amazing promises concerning the
future*. Verses 1:10-2:1 are an astounding and striking contrast to
the preceding verses. Sometimes God lets a relationship to him
'die' and then he raises it from the dead!

> **[10] But it shall be that the number of the people of Israel will be
> as the sand of the sea, which is not measured or numbered; and
> it shall be that in the place where it was said to them 'You are
> Lo-Ammi', it shall be said to them 'Sons of the living God'. [11]
> And the people of Israel and the people of Judah shall be gath-
> ered together, and they will appoint for themselves one head,
> and they shall go up from the land. Truly great is the day of
> Jezreel. [1] Say to your brothers 'Ammi', and to your sisters
> 'Ruhammah'.**

God will pick up with his people again and – despite the most savage and drastic chastenings by God – there will be a renewed Israel, with a renewed identity as God's people. God would pity them after all! Seven ingredients in the prediction may be noticed.

(i) *Numerical increase.* 'The number ... will be as the sand of the sea...'. The promises to Abraham concerning a vast multitude of 'children of Abraham' (see Genesis 13:16; 22:17) will be fulfilled, despite Israel's sin.

(ii) *Restoration of relationship.* 'In the place where it was said to them "You are Lo-Ammi", it shall be said to them "Sons of the living God".' 'The place' where this reversal of relationship takes place must be the northern territory of Israel in which Hosea ministered and where the sentence of their rejection (in 1:9) was issued. Reversal will take place in the same location.

(iii) *A new unity.* There would come a fulfilment of the hopes of unity across traditional enmities. The two nations 'shall be gathered together, and they will appoint for themselves one head'. Hosea 1:10b refers back to 1:8-9. Northern Israel ceased to be God's people, and for centuries the fellowship between God and his people in northern Israel was defunct. But, says Hosea, there will come an astonishing reversal.

The prediction would be fulfilled in stages. In the days of Hezekiah (729-687/6) some northerners joined Judah (2 Chronicles 30:11, 18), and Josiah treated the whole of Israel as under his reforming leadership (2 Chronicles 34:6-7, 9). Northerners sometimes settled in Judah (as 1 Chronicles 9:3 suggests). After the Babylonian exile (that is, after 538), the restoration of the nation was regarded as a time of restoration for believers from *both* kingdoms.

But a much richer fulfilment came. The ministry, death and resurrection of Jesus and the outpouring of the Holy Spirit involved special God-sent times of renewal for the Samaritans (see John 4:39) and there was an outpouring of the Holy Spirit specially for 'Samaria' – another name for northern Israel (Acts 8:4-17). The apostles were instructed to give Samaria special attention (Acts 1:8).

But there will be even greater fulfilments yet! Paul regarded the coming in of the gentiles as an extension of Hosea's predictions (Romans 9:24-26 quotes Hosea 1:10 and applies it to Gentiles). 'Israel' had Gentiles grafted into it! And there are yet fuller blessings to come as 'the full number of the Gentiles comes' and 'all Israel are saved' and 'life from the dead' (worldwide revival) comes upon the world (Romans 11:15, 25, 26).

The greatest means of unity in the church will always be the breath of God's reviving Holy Spirit. The people, again, 'shall be gathered together'.

(iv) *New headship.* Harmony arises by the two parts of the kingdom coming under a single Head. The united people of northern Israel and Judah would, said Hosea, 'appoint for themselves one head, and they shall go up from the land'. The 'head' is a reference to a coming 'Son of David'. From our point of view it is a reference to Jesus. The renewing gusts of life brought by God through the Holy Spirit would involve a new submission to God's King.

(v) *New exodus.* The words 'and they shall go up from the land' recalls the various times in Israel when they had 'gone up' from a place of bondage. The redemption from Egypt was the first, when the people of Israel 'went up' from the 'land of Egypt' (see Judges 19:30, and elsewhere; Hosea uses this vocabulary in 2:15). The restoration from Babylon would be another. The last sentence of 2 Chronicles mentions Cyrus' invitation to the people to 'go up' to Jerusalem. Ezra 7:7 tells us 'some ... went up'.

The word 'land' means 'land of exile'. Yet no specific place is mentioned and we may paraphrase the thought, 'They shall be brought out of wherever they are', 'they shall be rescued from whatever situation they are in'.

After Pentecost, the remnant of Israel 'went up' out of bondage as never before. Gentiles were grafted into remnant Israel; Hosea's prophecies were fulfilled further in the vast numbers of Gentiles that joined God's 'Israel'.

In the 'latter day glory' all the patterns of 'exodus' and 'restoration' will be fulfilled again. Even that will not be the end of it, for the day of Jesus' return will be an 'Exodus' from this world of sin, and a 'going up from the land'. Hosea was looking at northern Israel in his day. They were about to lose their national identity and for many centuries would not be God's people in any visible way. But Hosea is given to see a day when this would be reversed.

(vi) *A new starting-point.* A new meaning would be given to the word 'Jezreel', which means 'God sows'. Once it was associated with Jehu's murderous slaughter, but the blood of Jesus will speak better things than the blood of Jezreel. 'Truly great is the day of Jezreel'. Hosea sees that 'Jezreel' will one day take on another meaning. What God scattered in judgement, he would be ready to plant again. 'Jezreel' had meant 'God scatters'; it will come to mean 'God will take seed and plant them again and give them a new hope of fruitfulness and productivity'. The day of Israel's restoration, would be not an end but a starting point, not a reaping but a sowing. Romans 11:15 suggests the same thing: an *epoch* for a spiritually 'resurrected' people to serve God.

(vii) *Enjoyment of a new situation.* Just as, before, the adopted children of Hosea were to be saying to each other 'You are Not-Loved' or 'Your name is Not-My-People', now (in the symbolism) everything is reversed. One child says to another, 'You have a new name. Your new name is The-Loved-One.' Another child says, 'And your name is My-People.' Just as the children might rejoice in new names, so God's revived and restored Israel (eventually with Gentiles grafted into it) will rejoice in the consciousness that God has restored them.

Questions for Reflection

1. Can a church's relationship to God temporarily die?

2. How important are numbers in the Christian church?

3. In the light of Hosea 1, how is Christian unity encouraged?

3. Wayward Wife: Angry Husband (2:2-7)

In 2:2-23 the prophecy develops the symbolism that was presented to us in 1:2-9. The situation, in so far as it refers to Hosea and Gomer, is later than the time of 1:2-2:1. The children must rebuke the mother for her desertion of Hosea. The relationship between Hosea and Gomer has now been ruptured by Gomer's wrongdoing. No loving relationship exists between them at the moment.

But of course the passage is not primarily about Hosea and Gomer, although their story is visible and forms the background to what God says to Israel. Hosea's own story gave him insight into God's love, yet the themes of 2:2-23 focus on Israel more than on Gomer.

In 2:2-13 we have a section in which we are told of the sins of the wayward wife and the threats of the angry Husband. Gomer represents Israel; Hosea represents God. The section alternates between describing the behaviour of the wife and announcing the reaction of the husband.

1. The wife's behaviour: appeal to a wayward mother (verse 2).
2. What the husband will do: his discipline of the wife (verses 3-4).
3. The wife's behaviour: her harlotry (verse 5).
4. What the husband will do: forcing the woman home (verses 6-7).
5. The wife's behaviour, culpable ignorance (verse 8).
6. What the husband will do: therefore ... (verses 9-13).

Then the text moves again (in 2:14-23) from warnings to promises and from the immediate future to the long-distance future. For the moment we look at the first four alternating paragraphs.

First, we look at Gomer's behaviour (2:2). Hosea's *adopted* children must talk to their wayward mother.

> ² Argue with your mother, argue
> – for she is not my wife
> and I am not her husband –
> ³ lest I strip her naked ...

It must be remembered that Hosea has *two* groups of children.
Hosea 1:2 refers to those whom he was to adopt as his own. Hosea
1:3-9 refers to the two sons and one daughter who were fully his by
Gomer his wife. It will be noticed that Hosea 2:1 confirms this
understanding because it refers to more than one sister (changes
from the plural to the singular in some translations are unwarranted).
Hosea's marriage to Gomer led to the birth of only one girl, but the
'sisters' were among the adopted children of 1:2. Hosea was not
their father.

In the story of Hosea and Gomer, the relationship has soured.
The children are to confront their mother. The relationship is such
that Hosea is no longer a husband to Gomer. It does not mean that
a divorce has taken place but the relationship has failed. Gomer's
behaviour has necessarily shattered her closeness to Hosea. They
are no longer together as man and wife, and are not directly in
touch. Hosea sends a message via the children. The reference to
face and breasts seems to allude to a harlot's decorated face (see
Jeremiah 4:30; Ezekiel 23:40), while some bangle or bunch of
myrrh (see Song of Solomon 1:13) between the breasts signals her
availability to any man for a price. Hosea's wife had gone back to
her old ways; her sins were a combination of multiple adultery and
prostitution. But in taking such a step she has lost the *experience*
of Hosea's affection, although the affection itself was still there for
her if she could but have seen it.

The wantonness of Gomer recalled the behaviour of Israel. The
signs of devotion to Baal were evident in the land.

What is the modern equivalent? 'Baal' takes on different forms
in different ages. A generation ago it was what was called theological 'liberalism', a chop-suey mixture of scepticism and hu-
manism with bits of ex-Christian religiosity thrown in. It was a
suicidal religion and poisoned the churches that swallowed it. Today Baal in English-speaking churches has largely taken a different
form. One of its versions is a certain kind of consumer-friendly
mixture of entertainment and religious fund-raising with meetings that are more for the benefit of 'the ministry' than for the

kingdom of God. Old-style Pentecostalism and new-style charismatic movements have brought world-wide blessing and have led
millions into the kingdom of God. God has been at work even if
many mistakes have been made. Yet not every impulse and
impression we get is truly revelation from God, and the end of the
twentieth century is seeing some 'baals' arising from the worldwide blessing that began in the 1960s. The church of Jesus needs
to be ever alert both to see the genuine in the midst of many mistakes, and also to reject Satanic imitations in the midst of genuine
movements of the Spirit. Baal is a many-headed monstrosity and
can reappear in clever disguises.

Israel must face what the situation in the land really is. If Hosea's
children must confront their mother with the truth that she has lost
something in alienating Hosea, similarly Israel must face the fact
that they have forfeited God's blessing by alienating his goodwill.

*A second paragraph asks: what will Hosea do about his wayward
wife?* He invites her to abandon her prostitution and come home.
Otherwise he will take action:

> ... ³ lest I strip her naked,
>   and make her as on the day of her birth,
>   lest I make her like a wilderness,
>   lest I make her like a dry land,
>   and cause her to die of thirst.
> ⁴ To her children I will show no compassion,
>   for they are children of promiscuity.

False religion comes under God's judgement. The particular
judgements that Hosea mentions are disgrace and shame (2:3a),
dryness and thirst (2:3b), and disinterest and alienation from her
illegitimate children (2:4). The public humiliation of being stripped
naked was a fitting degradation, 'a saturation dose of her own
medicine'[8], doing to her publicly what she herself did privately. Sin

---

8. D. F. Kidner, *Love to the Loveless: The Message of Hosea* (IVP, 1981),
p. 28.

may be punished by our having more of it forced upon us. Israel
wanted to worship Assyrian gods; eventually she was sent to Assyria.
Hosea largely has Israel in mind. The nation will be humiliated
internationally. Far from being a land flowing with milk and honey,
it will be degraded with great humiliation, destitution, deprivation
and alienation from God himself.

In a third paragraph, Hosea returns to characterise the wife again.

> ⁵ **For their mother was a harlot;**
> **she who conceived them acted shamefully,**
> **for she said, 'I will go after my lovers,**
> **who gave me my bread and my water,**
> **my wool and my flax, my oil and my liquor.'**

I have suggested that some money-making strands of conservative
religion might be, or soon become, a modern Baal. Mercenary mo-
tives are quite obvious in some modern 'ministries'. Certainly it
was a leading factor in the religion of Hosea's day. Just as Gomer
was cultivating her customers not for their love but for their provi-
sions of flax, oil and wine, so the 'baals', the fertility gods of Israel,
were worshipped not in the interest of friendship with the gods but
in the hope of what could be got out of them. The baals promised a
very cosy life of agricultural fertility, scope for indiscriminate sex,
and a laid-back relationship with surrounding pagan society which
was imitated more than repudiated. Most people think that the purpose of 'faith' is to make life easier. The living God, however, ties
godliness and his provision for our lives together. 'All these things'
are indeed promised to us (Matthew 6:33), but they are the side-
effect of seeking first God's kingdom and righteousness. And the
Christian must be ready for the possibility of being 'the exception to
the rule' as Job was, the proof that godliness and prosperity do not
always go together.

But the Baal-worshippers wanted none of this. What was religion for – they thought – if not for 'my bread ... my water ... my
wool ... my flax, my oil ... my liquor'? The answers, 'my character

... my destiny ... my usefulness to God ... my hearing him say 'Well done' ... my eternal destiny', did not occur to them.

A fourth paragraph (2:6, 7) tells again of what Hosea, speaking for God, will do.

> **⁶ Therefore, behold, I will restrict her way with thornbushes,**
> **and I will fence her in with its walls,**
> **and she will not find her pathways.**
> **⁷ And she will pursue her lovers**
> **and will not overtake them.**
> **And she will seek them, but not find (them).**
> **And she may say, 'I will go back to my first husband,**
> **for it was better for me then than now'.**

God's chastening for Israel will involve restrictions and failures (2:6), lack of success in her chosen sinful path (2:7a) and eventually the painful process of being made wise by the experience of proving that the way of the sinner is hard (2:7b), and that God is a better husband than the 'lovers', the idols of the fertility cults.

God may obstruct our way by restrictions and failures. When he does so it may well be some kind of hint to us that he does not approve of the direction our lives are taking. If we find that our religion is being faced with thornbushes and our way is enclosed with guilt and failure, that in itself is a hint that God is pressurising us back to his ways. When our religiosity leads us into dismal failure, we ought to ask some questions.

Hosea holds out the prospect of Israel's being driven to God through sheer painful experience. Sometimes people genuinely and sincerely believe they can improve on the Christian faith. Perhaps something has disillusioned them or they have found no reality in the Christians they know and they turn to eastern religions or Marxism or they start 'living in the fast lane'. 'Old-fashioned Bible-religion is not for us', they say, as they pursue the modern gods. But the modern gods let us down as badly as the ancient baals. For many nations with a Christian past, the day may come when they will say, 'I will go

back to my first husband.' God has not initiated divorce proceedings.
The way is open to come back. When every way is hedged in
except the way back to God, it is no coincidence. The easy way to
know God is to heed his Word. The harder way is to discover that
the idols let us down, and do not bring us the blessings we seek
from them. Why should we be forced by painful experience into
saying, 'It was better for me then than now'? Israel did not learn at
this time. Verse 7 is best translated 'And she may say ...' rather
than 'And she will say'. At that time she did not repent. 'They
would not hear ... So Yahweh ... removed them' (2 Kings 17:14, 18)
and they went into exile never to come back to their old life again.

Better to be taught by God's Word than by the painfulness of
exile from his presence and his blessings.

Questions for Reflection

1. What aspects of the church should be called 'Baal' today?

2. Does 'Baal' change from age to age?

3. Is it possible to see God's action in the story of the church?

4. Naked Woman: Helpless Lovers (2:8-13)
Hosea 2:2-13 oscillates between picturing the wayward wife and
portraying the angry husband.

> Wayward wife: Hosea 2:2
> Angry husband: Hosea 2:3-4
> Wayward wife: Hosea 2:5
> Angry husband: Hosea 2:6-7

The pattern continues in Hosea 2:8-13, but the paragraph concerning the angry husband gets longer!

Wayward wife: Hosea 2:8
Angry husband: Hosea 2:9-13

The plural 'they' in verse 8 lets us know that the nation is more in mind that Gomer.

> **8 She does not know**
> **that I gave to her**
> **grain and the wine and the oil;**
> **the silver and gold, which I gave her in abundance,**
> **they used in order to make a Baal.**

The sin of the nation is wilful ignorance and gross misuse of God's gifts. The nation refused to allow that it was Yahweh who provided life's necessities. They believed the religious propaganda of the surrounding nations. 'If you want to get prosperity you must go to the baals' was the common idea. Yet the truth was, and still is, that God is as much in control of fertility as he is in control of salvation. He is the God of the earth as well as the God of heaven. Pledges of fertility for the land of Israel were built into God's covenant promises for the nation (Deuteronomy 7:13, 11:13-15; 26:1-11).

Israel made matters worse by misusing God's gifts. The very silver which was the sign of prosperity in Jeroboam's day was being used to make silver idols.

When the people of God turn away from him, the very things he gives them are misused. The money and the employment, the health and the prosperity which were given them by God are the very items they need in order to live godless lives.

Yet Israel had known God. It was no stranger that they were despising but one who had been, and wanted again to be, a Husband to the nation. Israel would not respond to God's questions and overtures of love.

Verses 9-13 give us a description of the wounded husband's response.

1. *There is the threat that the nation's prosperity will fail.*

> [9] Therefore I will turn around,
> and I will take away my grain in its time
> and my new wine in its seasons,
> and I will recover my wool and my flax,
> so as to uncover her nakedness.

The Hebrew word in the last line may be translated 'uncover', rather than the more common 'cover'.

God does not only punish in hell. His judgements fall in *this* world. The wrath of God *is* (now!) revealed, says the Bible (Romans 1:18). What we have in these verses is the reaction of a wounded Lover in a situation in which Israel has ceased to honour God as her divine Husband. The judgement consists of dismal failure, abysmal deprivation. God can bring his people into adversity in order to bring them back to himself.

God lets the false gods fail at the very point where they claim expertise. The claim of the baals was to provide fertility, yet God will bring drought and agricultural disaster of one kind or another. The result would be a failure of crops and vineyards, the death of wool-producing sheep. If the nation would not believe that obedience would lead to blessing, and idolatry would lead to deprivation, then they would eventually discover it when the sheer reality of deprivation would fall upon them.

Like a wife publicly deprived of her clothes, Israel would fall into disgrace. God had rescued the entire nation by the blood of the lamb. He had led them to Sinai to introduce them to a system of worship and of law which (for all its inadequacies, at that stage of salvation-history) took them in the direction of purity of life, and justice within the nation. Now Israel had abandoned a Redeemer-God and turned to gods of fertility and sexuality. But their worship of fertility and of sexuality brought them no blessings in the realm of fertility. The nation in fact became infertile and unproductive.

There are modern parallels. Little gods of unrestrained sexuality and of the worship of technology have had no effect at all in giving men and women peace or justice. The characteristics of northern Israel, its violence, its political instability, its religion or unrestrained sexuality – brought no blessings then and bring no blessings now.

2. *There is the threat that the nation's reputation will fail.*

> [10] **And now I will expose her lewdness**
> **in the sight of her lovers,**
> **and no one will rescue her from my hand.**

At one level this refers to what Hosea would do to Gomer. It seems to allude to a court process in which an immoral wife is stripped, exposed to public gaze as a punishment for her wickedness, and the lovers are helpless to do anything about it.

At another level it refers to what God will do to Israel. The nation would be disgraced. These are the people who were once so admired that the Queen of Sheba travelled a long distance to see their grandeur and then said, 'You have far exceeded the report I heard. How happy your men must be! ... Praise be to the LORD ... who has delighted in you ...' (1 Kings 10:7-9). But now the northern part of that very nation will be stripped and exposed like a disgraced harlot.

Part of God's blessings for our lives and for our nation is a good reputation. 'Glory' – the outshining of character – is part of God's reward. Conversely, God's punishments involve dishonour, the experience of shrinking in shame at his coming (contrast 1 John 2:28).

3. *There is the failure of her religion.*

> [11] **I will cause all her joy to cease,**
> **her feasts, her new-moon monthly celebrations, her sabbaths,**
> **and all her assemblies.**

Despite all of its sinfulness the nation of Israel thought of itself as very religious. It seems they also felt they were worshipping Yahweh. The nation's priests evidently felt that they were priests of Yahweh.

Centuries before, Jeroboam I (not Jeroboam II of Hosea's day) had introduced calves for worship and had said 'Here are your gods, O Israel, who brought you up out of the land of Egypt' (1 Kings 12:28). It was not that he was suggesting to the people that they worship another god. He simply brought in a 'new theology' of the God they already worshipped. But the 'new theology' was an idol.

So Israel was very religious. Attendance at worship was high. The people loved the festivals. Each new moon there were days of religious celebration.

But Israel's religion was not the faith of the Mosaic covenant. It was not the revelation given by Moses and the prophets. It may have used the language of the historic faith of Israel but it tangled the faith of Israel up in a mass of idolatry and careless living and disregard for God's written Word, the law of Moses.

When the Assyrians invaded, Israel's religion would be entirely useless to help them. The only spirituality that will be of any value to us is one that is God-given. Ritual and religiosity will be of no value. Traditional religion will not help, not even evangelical or charismatic religion. God will not be impressed, even by the newly introduced religious routines of yesterday. Nothing will stand when God acts, except that which has been introduced by God himself and is within his will. 'He that does the will of God will abide for ever.' Nothing else will survive, not even the religion that goes by his name.

4. *Another aspect of Israel's punishment involves disaster in the environment.* 'Ecology' and 'environmental science' have been world-wide concerns in recent years. Yet biblical revelation has always tied together the well-being of 'nature' and the obedience of men and women to God. When God created the world, he created it for men and women. When humankind fell, creation fell. When humankind was redeemed creation was redeemed. Humanity and creation have always been tied together. 'Nature' is affected when men and women sin.

Because of Israel's idolatry, God says,

> [12] **I shall lay waste her vines and her fig-trees,**
> **about which she said,**
> **'They are my wages which my lovers gave me.'**
> **And I shall make them into a forest**
> **and animals of the countryside shall devour them.**

It is a picture of ecological disaster. Vines and fig-trees are damaged. The very fertility that Israel felt was the salary for her worship of the baals now discontinues. Vineyards become overrun with weeds and revert to being wild forests. Animals take over what once was enjoyed by men and women.

In parts of the world where factories and technology are conspicuous, our dependence on the 'fertility' of the world is taken for granted. But in the less industrialised nations the truth is nearer at hand to be observed. The truth is, our world is rapidly moving towards ecological crisis. Along with unmanageable populations, overgrazing and deforestation characterise many parts of the world. Whereas Israel's judgement might involve a surfeit of animals, the modern crisis involves loss of species and depletion of the world's population of animals, birds and trees. A major part of the cause is greed and worldwide inequalities. 'Aid' organisations can do little unless the donors, the mediators and the receivers are men and women of integrity. The crisis is spiritual. Ungodliness still has ecological side-effects.

5. *There is the failure of her future.*

> [13] **And I will punish her for the days of the baals,**
> **to whom she burnt incense,**
> **and she decked herself with nose-ring and necklace**
> **and went after her lovers – but she forgot me.**
> >   **Oracle of Yahweh.**

The nation is held responsible for the way it has been guilty of spiritual adultery in worshipping the gods of fertility, and seeking their favours. The nation has been like a harlot dressing up for her lovers.

The deeper sin has been forgetfulness of Yahweh. Men and women are incurably religious. When they reject the God of the Bible they end up going after some degraded god. In some parts of the English-speaking world, the worship of the God of the Bible has diminished, but the result has not been atheism. Rather, men and women have turned to astrology, 'new age' theosophy, and the like. The new gods provide nothing worth having; the tragedy is that the only God, whose worship leads to purity and happiness, is forgotten.

These verses are Hosea's analysis, under God's illumination, of the situation in northern Israel. It is not his last word. Hosea 2:14-23 will turn from analysis to hope. There will be a 'door of hope' (2:15). They will yet be married to Yahweh 'in righteousness and in justice' (2:19).

But Hosea puts analysis before optimism. The seriousness of the situation in Hosea's day must be realised. If some will see it and seek Yahweh, 'the door of hope' is open right now.

Questions for Reflection

1. In what ways does God punish in this world?

2. What is the difference between religion and spirituality?

3. What is the connection between godliness and ecology?

5. Paradise Regained (2:14-23)
Just as Hosea 1:2-9 was followed by the positive message of 1:10-2:1, so Hosea 2:2-13 is followed by the promises of 2:14-23.

First there is the promise of *a new courtship* (14-15).

> **¹⁴ Therefore behold I will allure her**
> **and bring her to the wilderness**
> **and I will speak tenderly to her.**
> **¹⁵ And I will give her her vineyards there,**
> **and the valley of Achor as a door of hope,**

and she will respond there as in the days of her youth
and as in the day of her going up from the land of Egypt.

The time of the wanderings in the wilderness (1280-1240 BC roughly), after Israel was saved from Egypt, was a relatively obedient time for Israel. It is not that Israel was 100% pure but the nation responded with faith. There were no rivals to God. True, there were lapses (see Exodus 32:1-6), but the nation was relatively faithful until the idolatry of Solomon (1 Kings 11:4-8) brought disaster.

But God is capable of recalling his people despite the most awful decline. He will take the initiative ('I will allure ... I will bring ... I will give ...').

The first major disobedience in Israel's story came, at about 1240 BC, as Israel was invading Canaan under the leadership of Joshua. Achan stole some of the idolatrous objects that were meant to be destroyed, and was executed in the valley of Achor (Joshua 7:24, 26).

But God promises he will reverse all of this. Instead of Achor and disobedience and idolatry, God will work powerfully among his people taking the initiative to bring them back to himself. And they will respond! It will be as if God were taking the nation back into the days when he redeemed it by the blood of the lamb. He will bring the nation into the wilderness again. When it faces up to the challenge as the Israelites faced the challenge of Achor, the wilderness will become a place of hope.

Second, there is the promise of *a new purity of faith* (16-17).

[16] **And it shall be on that day – oracle of Yahweh –**
you shall call me 'My husband'
and you shall not call me any more 'My baal'.
[17] **And I will take away the names of the baals from her mouth,**
and they shall not be remembered any more by their name.

Like many today, northern Israel had a muddled view of Yahweh. The fertility gods were often identified with Yahweh himself, and Yahweh himself was often called 'my baal'. People who do not know God often say 'All religions are really the same. We all worship God.' In the same way, Israel would talk as if Yahweh, the God of redemption by the blood of a lamb, was another form of the baals who offered a mixture of erotic rituals and agricultural prosperity. Jeroboam I regarded his idols as a representation of Yahweh (1 Kings 12:28). The people thought of the worship of Yahweh and the worship of the baals as one thing. The priests of northern Israel evidently regarded themselves as Yahweh's priests. The festivals were festivals to Yahweh. The word 'baal' was very convenient for this muddled religion, which mixed up faith in Yahweh with allegiance to the immoral gods of the Canaanites.

The fact that the Christian faith, Hinduism and Islam (to choose some random examples) all use the word 'god' beguiles the unwary into thinking, 'All these religions worship God; they are just different version of the same thing.' No, not so! They use the *word* 'god', but what they worship is different in each case. To use a word in common is not to have a faith in common.

'Baal' means 'lord' or 'owner'. It could be used of Yahweh, for Yahweh was the Lord and owner of the universe. 'Baal' could quite innocently be used to refer to the one and only God of all creation and of Israel. 'Baal' also has the meaning 'husband', and it is true that Yahweh is a heavenly Lover, a Husband. It is also true that God is the source of fertility. But pagan beliefs liked to take this imagery and exploit it to produce a religion of its own, where this language was made into erotic ritual. A religion which offered easy sex and material prosperity was a spicy and popular concoction. If the name 'Yahweh' could be used, it seemed to be showing loyalty to Israel's ancient faith and would please people who were old-fashioned enough to remember Israel's story of how the nation originated. One thinks of certain eastern religions which are happy to add 'Jesus' to their list of gods just to please the Christians! But the Jesus who is 'one name in a list' is, of course, not the Jesus of the Bible.

Hosea predicts that this religious cocktail will one day be swept away. The worship of Yahweh would no longer be confused with the religion of the baals. The living, righteous, holy God, who saves by the blood of a Substitute, would be worshipped in spirit and in truth. The people of God will – says Hosea – regard Yahweh, and Yahweh alone, as 'husband'. And he will not be muddled with the baals. 'You shall not call me any more "My Baal"'. Idolatry will be abolished. God will be rightly named. Other gods will be forgotten, and Yahweh alone will be worshipped among God's people.

Third, in Hosea's prophetic vision, there is the promise *of a new covenant* (18-20).

> [18] And I will cut for them a covenant in that day,
> with the animals of the countryside
> and with the birds of the sky,
> and with the reptiles of the ground.
> And I will remove out of the earth
> the bow and the sword and the weapons of battle;
> and I will cause them to lie down in safety.
> [19] And I shall betroth you unto me for ever;
> I shall betroth you to me in righteousness and in justice,
> in devotion and in compassion.
> [20] I shall betroth you to me in faithfulness;
> then you shall know Yahweh.

A 'covenant' is a special kind of pledge, a promise that has been made unbreakably binding (at least in theory) by the taking of an oath. In the story of the woman of Tekoa (2 Samuel 14) we see how she persuades David to turn a casual promise (2 Samuel 14:8) into an oath-bound promise. 'As Yahweh lives ...' (2 Samuel 14:11) is a formula for swearing with an oath. Once the woman has got the king to take an oath, that is, to make a covenant, he cannot change his mind.

In such a way God promises an all-embracing restoration to a perfection which is like that of Eden. There will be a new earth (verse 18), characterised by peace and prosperity (verse 18). There will be a new marriage-relationship between God and his people (verse 19), a new knowledge of the LORD (verse 20).

Predictive prophecy generally has a *panoramic* viewpoint. In many of the cities of the world you find some kind of tall building or tower. There is the Eiffel tower of Paris, the Hillbrow tower of Johannesburg, the Kenyatta International Conference Centre of Nairobi, and so on. From the top of these structures you get a sweeping view of the city below and of the surrounding country-side. You look in one direction and see the nearby valleys. You look in another direction and see a distant mountain. You look below and see the city with its traffic and its pedestrians. You can see an unusual building over there, a football stadium here. You see the sun shining from one direction and the clouds of impending rain in another direction. You can see everything! It is one sweeping viewpoint, a panorama, a total overview, a vista.

Old Testament prophecy is rather like that. It starts from where the prophet is and it looks out on a total 'panorama' of everything that God will do. Its horizon stretches into the unimaginably   dis-tant future. Just as from a tall building you can see the streets below and the mountains a hundred miles away, so the prophets see what God is about to do and they see where he will take his people to in the distant future.

The vast panorama gets fulfilled in stages. There would be the restoration under Ezra and Nehemiah. In further centuries, there would be the coming of Jesus and the sending out of the apostles into Jerusalem, then into Judea and into Samaria, and then into the 'uttermost parts of the earth'. There would be the spreading of the gospel of Jesus into every corner of the globe. And as I understand the matter, there is yet to be a greater measure of spiritual blessing for the people of God, namely, the maturity of the church, the reach-ing of all nations, the conversion of Israel, 'life from the dead' (Romans 11:15) at a worldwide level. And that still will not be the end, for there will eventually be the new heavens and the new earth in which dwells righteousness.

The prophets stood on an 'Eiffel tower' and were given glimpses of all that God would do: the coming of a new King David, spiritual revival, restoration for Israel (into which Gentiles would be incorporated). But included in the 'panorama' is the vision of earthly glory. God is utterly 'covenanted' to doing this. He cannot change his mind.

Fourth, there is the promise of a *new harmony* (2:21-23).

> [21] And it shall happen on that day;
> I shall respond (it is an oracle of Yahweh!)
> I shall respond to the heavens and they shall respond to the earth.
> [22] And the earth will respond to the grain and the wine and the oil;
> and they will respond to Jezreel.
> [23] And I shall sow her to me in the land,
> and I shall pity Lo-Ruhamma;
> and I shall say to Lo-Ammi 'You are my people'
> and he will say 'My God'.

The promise includes a new harmony between God and the earth (2:21-22) and between God and Israel (verse 23). This is what the people of Israel were interested in – earthly prosperity! It will come, but not through the baals. It will come, but it cannot be switched on in a few seconds of religious ritual.

The Bible's picture of final glory is not the medieval picture of angels floating around in space. It is men and women in glorified bodies in a glorified world. It is a picture of the skies sending rain to the earth, and the very land beneath our feet becoming productive as never before. The whole of Israel becomes 'Jezreel' ('God sows'), an exhibition of what God can plant in human lives. Israel becomes 'Pitied' – the object of God's restoring compassion. The nation again becomes 'Ammi', a nation of people who use the words 'My God' because God is known and loved.

It is all fulfilled in Jesus. Gentiles can come into it, because the gates of 'Israel' are open to all who share Abraham's faith. It is being brought to consummation. In the end it will continue for ever for those who love God.

Questions for Reflection

1. How is courtship like God's seeking his people?

2. How does it affect our reading of the Old Testament to know that prophecy is 'panoramic'?

3. Is prophecy ever fulfilled in stages?

6. Hosea's Love and God's Love (3:1-5)

We have seen how Hosea's marriage started (1:2-9). We have deduced from Hosea 2:2-13 how it deteriorated when Gomer turned again to the evil habits of her former days. Now Hosea 3:1-5 points to a later stage in the relationship when Gomer's position had deteriorated yet further. The predictions of Hosea 2 had come to pass in the life of Gomer. Her financial resources had run dry; her men-friends had not brought her the income she sought. The promises of her lovers had not come to fruition. Perhaps her lifestyle resulted in the loss of her earlier attractiveness. A life of late nights and loose morals would bring its physical side effects, to say nothing of the diseases that would come with her way of living and loving. Now she is in a desperate plight.

How would most husbands have reacted to all of this? How would most Christian husbands respond? How would I? Most would surely react with bitterness ('I hate her for what she did'), vindictiveness ('She got what she deserved'), self-righteousness ('How could she do a thing like that?'). Perhaps we would have lost many nights' sleep and would have gone over and over what she had done. I think I would have given up on her, and written her off as a hopeless case! Many men would have wallowed in regrets over the past. 'Why did I ever marry her in the first place?' any one of us might have said.

But then, many of us would have recovered eventually. Many abandoned husbands would perhaps go away for a holiday, move house, change jobs, get some new friends, find another woman, and bury the memory of Gomer, regarding her as a part of their lives best forgotten! Maybe this is what Hosea would have done, except that God spoke to him.

Hosea 3:1-5 does not tell us much, but it hints that Gomer had fallen into slavery; Hosea buys her out of her plight at the market value of a slave.

> [1]**And Yahweh said to me again, 'Go love a woman already loved by a companion, an adulteress – just as Yahweh loves the Israelites, but they turn to other gods, and love cakes of raisins.'**

We begin to see the love of God when we realise that God was faced with a people who might have brought him some regrets! The people gave 'cakes of raisins', cooked offerings to a female deity, the 'queen of heaven' (see Jeremiah 7:18; 44:19).

Hosea took in hand the matter of his fallen wife with boldness and confidence. He was not a weeping cuckold.

> [2] **So I bought her for myself with fifteen pieces of silver, a 'homer' of barley and a 'letek' of barley. [3]And I said to her, 'For many days you will wait for me. You will not be promiscuous; and you shall not belong to any man. Then indeed I will be yours'.**

Hosea (i) paid the price necessary to get his wife back ('So I bought her...'), (ii) put her in a restricted situation for a long time ('For many days you will wait ...You will not be promiscuous... you shall not belong to any man...'). Gomer, the former slave-concubine of someone else but now redeemed, was allowed no sexual relationship with anyone, not even her husband, until she had come to a change of heart. Then, (iii) Hosea gave himself to her and insisted that he would never let her go ('Then indeed I will be yours').

Hosea paid a mixture of money and food to get back his wife. 'Homer' and 'letek' are measures of weight. God plans to do something similar for Israel.

(i) He will *pay the price necessary to get his people*. Throughout the Bible the thought is often presented that God 'buys' his people at great cost to himself. Apparently Gomer had become someone's slave-concubine. The price Hosea paid was roughly the price that was spent in redeeming slaves.[9] God does the same thing. Sin sets up a bondage. Northern Israel had becomes slaves to their immoral gods and were so entrenched in sin that even God had to 'pay a price' to get the nation released. Often in the Bible the 'price' is simply the great lengths to which God will go. The Bible does not envisage God as saving us with effortless ease. Yahweh's action is at cost to himself. He buys us out of bondage 'with a stretched out arm' (Exodus 6:6). The theme of price-paying is taken further in the New Testament when we discover that redemption is at the cost of Jesus' blood.

(ii) *God will put his people in Israel into a restricted situation.*

⁴ For during many days the Israelites will wait without king and without prince and without sacrifice and without pillar and without ephod or teraphim.

We recall that Hosea's ministry began in about 760 BC. If this oracle was given after (at a guess) eight years of marriage at about 752, then the nation had about 25 years left before 723, when the Assyrians destroyed Samaria and brought the northern kingdom of Israel to an end. Then 'during many days' the territory would have no king. In fact Israel has never had a king since.

For many days it would be 'without sacrifice'. Northern Israel was scattered. There would be no temple-worship, no sacrificial system, for centuries. To this day Israel has no system of animal-sacrifices.

For many days it would be 'without pillar'. The 'pillar' was the upright standing stone commemorating some aspect of one's experience with God or with the gods. They had once been used

---

9. See Wolff, *Hosea*, p. 61.

innocently (see e.g. Genesis 28:18) but now were part of Israel's depraved worship.

For many days it would be 'without ephod'. The 'ephod' was some kind of waistcoat in which there were pockets. In origin it was innocent and was required by the Mosaic law for God's true priests, but it could easily be corrupted and become a garment for an image. Judges 8:24-28 illustrates the point.

For many days the nation would be 'without teraphim'. The 'teraphim' were small images, household gods. The word is plural ('teraphs'). These statuettes had no lawful place in Israel's worship and always were associated with menacing idolatry.

(iii) *He will give himself to his people and insist that he will never let them go.*

> **⁵ Afterwards, the Israelites will turn and seek Yahweh their God and David their king. They will come trembling to the LORD and to his blessings at the end of the age.**

Hosea the prophet is enabled to know that just as he had dealt with his wife severely so as eventually to bring about a restored relationship, God would do the same in the future story of his relationship to Israel.

He is looking into the distant future ('Afterwards ... at the end of the age'). The prophecy of Hosea has a two-phase view of the future. The immediate future is bleak; their only hope lies in immediate repentance. But Hosea predicts future blessing. The Israelites will turn to God, and will seek him. A new 'David' will come. The original David had ruled over the united people of God, Israel and Judah. He was chosen by God, anointed by the Spirit. He hated idolatry, loved God, and was a man after God's own heart.

Hosea predicts a new 'David' will come. He too will rule over God's people everywhere. He too will do his work in the power of the Holy Spirit. Through him the people of Israel – restructured and with Gentiles incorporated – would come trembling in repentance and with an eagerness never to fall again. The things that

Israel lost would be restored to them in Jesus. Jesus would be their king. Jesus would be Israel's sacrifice. Jesus would be their pillar – the One who endlessly reminded them of what God had done for them. Jesus would be their ephod, their Guide, their means of knowing God's will. Jesus would even be their 'image' of God, for he is indeed 'the image of the invisible God'. And 'Israel' would become like the sand of the seashore with Gentiles engrafted into God's people to become fellow-citizens with the holy people and members of the household of God. For the Christian the fulfilment of the prophecy has started; our 'David' has come. But there is more, and we can expect greater blessings yet.

The point of the story is the greatness of God's love. God was deeply committed to his people. Just as Hosea knew from the beginning what sort of woman he was getting, so God knows what sort of people he is taking when he takes us, his 'Israel'. The sins of the nation caused no great surprise to God, nor do the sins of Israel in its modern re-structured form as the church.

God had committed himself to a wicked people. Israel had no 'genius for religion' (as is sometimes said). The nation had a genius for backsliding! But God was not taken by surprise and had no plan to let his people go or fail to fulfil his plans for the world through the nation.

God's love will take the effort that is needed and pay the price that needs to be paid. 'Yahweh loves the Israelites', says Hosea. No matter what they have done, he will not leave his people or forsake them. They are engraved on the palms of his hands. Nothing and no one will separate them from his love, not even their own inbred foolishness.

God will succeed in bringing his people where he wants them to be. He takes a long time. With nations he takes centuries. But eventually he gets his will done. 'For many days you will wait ... Then indeed I will be yours.'

Both with individuals and with his 'Israel', God takes his time but gets his will done. He does not force our wills but he so works in our circumstances and even amidst extreme hardships so as to get us back. He works persistently and with great wisdom and care until we 'come trembling to Yahweh and his goodness'.

The modern Christian, by his faith in Jesus, is part of this 'Israel'. The church of Jesus Christ is the believing, elect sub-section of the nation of Israel, reduced to a remnant, but with large numbers of Gentiles grafted into it. 'If you are Christ's then you are Abraham's seed' (Galatians 3:29).[10]

But one day Israel 'according to the flesh' will abandon its unbelief and become part of 'Israel' according to the Holy Spirit. Nothing can separate us from the love of God in Christ Jesus. Nothing, not even our own sins.

Questions for Reflection

1. Does love have to be tough?

2. Does God ever withdraw love in order to bless us?

3. In what ways is Jesus a 'new David'?

---

10. For the relationship between Israel and the church, see M.A. Eaton, *How To Enjoy God's Worldwide Church* (Sovereign World, 1995), chapter 4.

2

The Message of Hosea Elaborated
(4:1-14:9)

7. Three Catastrophes In Israel (4:1-3)

Chapters 4-13 take up fuller details of Hosea's preaching. Hosea
4:1-3 is an appropriate beginning; it focuses on the central indict-
ment of the nation. God has a dispute with the nation (4:1a). Three
essentials of society were missing (4:1b). Major crimes were sweeping
the nation (4:2) and the countryside was suffering as a result.

> [1] **Hear the word of Yahweh, O people of Israel.**
> **For Yahweh has a controversy with the inhabitants of the land.**
> **For there is no faithfulness and no mercy**
> **and no knowledge of God in the land.**
> [2] **Swearing and lying and murdering and stealing and commit-**
> **ting adultery!**
> **They break all bounds, and with bloodshed upon bloodshed they**
> **strike people down.**
> [3] **Therefore the land dries up**
> **and all the inhabitants in it languish,**
> **with the animals of the countryside and with the birds of heaven,**
> **and also the fish of the sea are cleared away.**

Let us consider first the three great needs of the nation.

1. *The land was in need of 'faithfulness'.* The Hebrew word (*'emet*)
includes such ideas as accuracy, honesty, sincerity, reliability,
faithfulness, steadfastness. It is often used of God's faithfulness,
his truthfulness in fulfilling promises, and his loyalty to men and
women (Genesis 24:27; 32:10). The thought of God's genuineness
and faithfulness towards us is often mentioned in prayer. 'You have
dealt faithfully', said the people of Israel to God (Nehemiah 9:33).
'All the paths of the LORD are lovingkindness and faithfulness' (Psalm
25:10). 'Your words are truth, and you have promised this good
thing...', said David (2 Samuel 7:28). 'The judgements of the LORD
are true' (Psalm 19:9).

But men and women were made in the image of God, and 'truth'
is also required of them. When Abraham's servant said that he
knew God to be a God of 'lovingkindness and faithfulness' (Gen-

esis 24:27), he asked the same thing from Laban's family to whom he was speaking (verse 49). Jacob asked the same thing from Joseph (Genesis 47:29). Rahab asked the spies to give her a 'pledge of faithfulness', something that would show her their intention to be merciful towards her (Joshua 2:12). They gave a promise that they would deal with her in kindness and faithfulness (verse 14). The word means trustworthiness, faithfulness. Nehemiah put somebody in charge of the work of God because 'he was a faithful man' (Nehemiah 7:2).

'Truth' is supremely to be the characteristic of speaking or of words. The words of Joseph's brothers were tested as to 'whether there is truth' in them (Genesis 42:16). A king asked a prophet to speak 'nothing but the truth' (1 Kings 22:16; 2 Chronicles 18:15). The widow of Zarephath came to be sure that God's words in the mouth of Elijah were 'truth' (1 Kings 17:24). Mordecai sent letters that had words of peace and truth. They were designed to spread peace, well-being. But they were also true. They kept to the facts. They were trustworthy, genuine (Esther 9:30). The psalmist speaks of the blessing that comes upon the person who 'speaks the truth' (Psalm 15:2).

Hosea's concern is especially with Israelite society. 'Truth' was specially required of civic officials. At the beginning of the nation's history Moses required that the judges of Israel be 'men of truth' (Exodus 18:21). Joshua urged the people to serve God in wholeheartedness and in 'truth', that is to say, in faithfulness, in firm commitment to God. (Joshua 24:14). David urged the same thing upon Solomon concerning his descendants (2 Kings 2:4).

'Truth' also includes the idea of sincerity. In the parable of the trees in Judges 9, the bramble speaks of what is true 'If in sincerity, genuineness you are anointing me as king ... If you have dealt in truth – in sincerity – and in integrity ... if you have dealt in genuineness ...' (verses 5, 16, 19). We are to serve God 'in genuineness,' said Samuel (1 Samuel 12:24).

2. *The land needed to show kindly mercy within its society.* The Hebrew word here (*chesed*) is again the word that can be used both of God and of man. It may be translated 'lovingkindness' when it refers to God's character. When referring to human character and conduct it is 'merciful kindness' and includes 'generous and forgiving treatment that makes coexistence possible'. It is a mixture of judgement and mercy, 'producing a blend of retribution and forgiveness which constitutes ... justice'.[11]

Lot was shown kindness by God when God rescued him from the destruction of a sinful city (Genesis 19:19). God showed Abraham 'steadfast love' in leading his servant to Isaac's wife (Genesis 24:12, 14, 27). God showed 'lovingkindness' to Joseph in prison (Genesis 39:21). God's guidance comes because of his lovingkindness (Exodus 15:13). It is specially given to those who keep his commandments (Exodus 20:6; Deuteronomy 7:9,12). It is part of the glory of his love, in combination with God's mercy, graciousness, slowness to anger (Exodus 34:6). It is his kindness that leads him to forgive the sins of thousands (Exodus 34:7; Deuteronomy 5:10).

The word is often combined with 'faithfulness'. Abraham's servant speaks of God's 'lovingkindness and faithfulness' (Genesis 24:27) and he asked Laban to deal with him in 'kindness and faithfulness'. The two words together have a balancing effect. What is the good of being faithful if there is no kindness? Some people are so kind they do not tell the truth. They lie to be kind! Others are faithful to the truth but show no kindness. Kindness and faithfulness balance each other.

The word means 'kindly favour', even in the sense of the English phrase 'to do someone a favour'. Abraham asked Sarah to 'do him an act of kindness' in pretending to be Abraham's sister (Genesis 20:13). Joseph asked the cupbearer of Pharaoh for a 'favour' (Genesis 40:14). See also Genesis 47:29. Yet, although 'lovingkindness' goes beyond anything that is deserved, it must be

---

11. Andersen & Freedman, *Hosea*, p.336.

noticed that there are places where it is a response to someone's obedience or to their own kindnesses.

When used of the kindness of men and women towards each other, the word has the sense of love, mercy, mutual loyalty. Abimelech says to Abraham: 'As I have dealt in kindness towards you, you deal with me in the same way...' (Genesis 21:23). As this passage indicates, *chesed* often has the idea of 'mutual kindness' or 'loyalty to one another'. 'Since I have dealt with you in kindness,' said Rahab to the spies, 'you deal with my father's house in kindness' (Joshua 2:12). The spies reply, 'Our life for yours!' and promise Rahab she will be dealt with in kindness appropriate to the kindness she has shown them (2:14). The word can also mean 'devotion', loyalty to God, faithfulness to him, as in Hosea 6:6.

A society that wanders away from 'devotedness' towards God, *chesed*, begins to lack kindly mercy or merciful kindness, *chesed*, towards fellow human beings.

In the book of Hosea the word comes six times. In Hosea 2:19 God promised that he would one day 'betroth' Israel to himself for ever. 'I shall betroth you to me in righteousness and in justice, with *mercy* and with compassion'. The characteristics seem to refer both to what God is like, and to what the people will be like. It will be a marriage relationship which on all sides is characterised by kindness. But Israelite society is far from being like that at the point where Hosea was ministering. So here in Hosea 4:1-3 we have a definitive statement of what is lacking in Israelite society. It was bereft of kindly mercy, merciful kindness. In chapter 6:4 and 6, Hosea will return to the same point: 'Your *loyalty* to me is like a morning cloud ... I delight in *mercy* rather than sacrifice...'. The nation needs to 'reap ... in mercy' (10:12), to 'observe mercy' (12:6).

3. *The land needed the knowledge of God.* Sometimes 'knowledge' means 'practical know-how' and is linked with skill and craftsmanship (Exodus 31:3; 35:31; 1 Kings 7:14), and sometimes it is knowledge of facts (Deuteronomy 4:42; 19:4; Joshua 20:3,

20:5), but here Hosea has in mind understanding, wisdom, spiritual insight (Job 13:2; 15:2; 33:3). God has such knowledge supremely. Know-ledge of spiritual things comes by God's direct teaching. He teaches people knowledge (Psalm 94:10), gives proverbs and say-ings to impart knowledge (Proverbs 22:25) and calls upon us to apply our minds to instruction (Proverbs 23:12). God's people pray for it (Psalm 119:66). Spiritual knowledge is part of wisdom and part of righteous living. The fear of Yahweh is its beginning (Prov-erbs 1:7; 9:10). Fools hate it (Proverbs 1:22, 29), and know nothing of it (Proverbs 14:7; 29:7). Men and women of loose morals have none of it (Proverbs 5:2). Wise people seek it (Proverbs 2:5; 15:14), acquire it (Proverbs 18:15,15); are willing to face reproof to get it (Proverbs 19:25), and want instruction in order to get it (Proverbs 21:11). They lay it up as treasure (Proverbs 10:14; 20:15). It floods the life of the wise person and is pleasant to him (Proverbs 2:10; 24:4, 5).

The greatest 'knowledge' is 'knowledge of the Most High' (Num-bers 24:16). This involves knowledge of God personally, and knowl-edge of God's 'ways' (Job 21:14; Isaiah 58:2).

There is a knowledge which is indispensable. 'My people go into exile for lack of knowledge', said Isaiah (Isaiah 5:13). Hosea grieved for the nation's lack of knowledge (4:1), denounced the priests for its absence (. 4:6) and said 'knowledge of God' was a supreme requirement (6:6). Malachi made similar points (Malachi 2:7).

Knowledge of God is not purely factual. It is awareness and experience of God Himself. It involves righteousness and com-passion. It is to judge the cause of the poor and needy. 'Is not this to know me?' asks God (Jeremiah 22:16).

But instead of faithfulness, mercy and the knowledge of God, there was in Hosea's time an abundance of crime. 'Swearing' means malicious cursing of other people. It is a breach of the third commandment. 'Lying, murdering, stealing and committing adultery' are transgressions of the ninth, sixth, eighth and seventh of the ten commandments of Exodus 20:1-17, respectively.

Israelite society was riddled with violence, deceit and impurity of every kind. Two centuries before, the first Jeroboam had introduced idolatry into Israel. Even the powerful ministries of Elijah and Elisha had not turned the country around permanently. Two hundred years later, in Hosea's time, the social consequences are unmistakable. Rejection of the God of the Bible will affect society. The decay may be slow but it will be steady. A generation will perhaps reject God's revelation but want to hold on to morality and decency or at least safety in the streets and in their home. But when God's self-revelation is rejected sin grows in power and soon will be open, obvious. Society becomes riddled with deceit, violence, impurity, theft. The seed was rejection of God; the fruit is social decay. Then, even nature is affected. Hosea 4:3 implies a formidable drought. God is rejected first, then society is affected. Then the very environment, even the very air we breath, is all affected by man's sinful ways. Nothing can stop the steady consequences of sin except faith in God who 'makes bare his mighty arm' to save us.

Questions for Reflection

1. In what areas of our society is there special need of mercy?

2. How does the fear of the Lord promote knowledge?

3. If God's dealings with a country take centuries how has God been dealing with our country over the last century?

8. A Priest's Family (4:4-10a)
The Hebrew of Hosea 4:4-19 is obscure. This is one of the places in the Hebrew Bible where it is best to seek to improve the medieval 'Massoretic' pointing and to make better sense of the passage than the Massoretes did (see pages 16-20 above).

Let us consider the five places where the text is difficult. Then we shall come back to the message of the passage as a whole. Those who do not wish to trouble themselves with technicalities of translation can skip the next five paragraphs if they wish!

1. In verse 4 one attempt to make sense of the Massoretic text goes like this.

> Let no man strive, and let no man rebuke,
> And your people are like those who strive with a priest.

However, the word 'those who strive' probably does not exist! With some tiny rewriting of the vowel-points (which it must be remembered were added only in early medieval times) it could be read as follows:

> **⁴ Surely God has a controversy with a certain person.**
> **And there is a person God reproves.**
> **With you surely is my controversy, O priest!**

This is much more likely. The Hebrew word '*al* ('not') is twice read as '*el* ('God'); the two words are the same except for the vowel. And the emended translation reads *we 'immeka* ('and with you') instead of *we 'ammeka* ('and your people'), and *kimma ribi* ('surely...my controversy') instead of *kimeribe* ('like those who strive with'?). The translation I follow does not emend the MT. It simply reads a different set of vowel-points.

2. The next troublesome line is in verse 7. The MT might be translated:

> ⁷ As they became great, so they sinned against me. Their glory I
> will change into their shame.

But if '*amir* ('I will change') is read as '*amiru* ('they changed'), a better translation is obtained.

[7] **As they became great, so they sinned against me.**
Their glory they changed into their shame.

3. The next tricky piece of Hebrew text is in verses 10-12. In verse
10 the Massoretic Text could be translated:

> [10] They have eaten but will not be satisfied. They have been promis-
> cuous but will not increase. They have forsaken Yahweh, to keep....

But the verse in the MT seems to have no sensible ending. 'To
keep' what? Then verse 11 in the Massoretic Text goes like this:

> [11] Harlotry, wine and new wine take away the heart.

And the MT of verse 12 reads:

> My people, from his piece of wood, he makes enquiry...

All of this is very obscure, but with a little patience and close attention it does make sense. The word 'harlotry' probably does 'double
duty'. The one word belongs at the end of verse 11 and also at the
beginning of verse 12. Also the first word of verse 12 probably
belongs in verse 11. So we may read it like this.

> [10]**They have eaten but will not be satisfied.**
> **They have been promiscuous but will not increase.**
> **They have forsaken Yahweh to keep harlotry.**
> [11] **Harlotry, wine and new wine take away the heart** [12] **of my**
> **people.**
> **He makes enquiry from his wood; and his staff reports to him.**
> **For by a spirit of promiscuity he has led people astray.**
> **And they act promiscuously in defiance of their God.**

4. Verse 14 is often translated:

> I will not punish your daughters
> when they commit harlotry.
> Nor your daughters-in-law
> when they commit adultery.

But if the MT word for 'not' (*lo*') is taken as the Hebrew word for 'surely' (*lu*') it reads more sensibly. The verb is always used to announce punishment in Hosea. Or, if one wishes to retain the 'not', it would be best to take it as a question, 'Shall I not...?' Either way, Hosea is speaking of judgement, not of the women *escaping* judgement, which would not fit Hosea's thought at all. Later in the verse there is a word (the Hebrew emphasizing-*ki*) which should be translated 'actually'; and the Hebrew pronoun is masculine and has to refer to men.

So the verse should read:

¹⁴ I will surely send punishment upon your daughters because
they are promiscuous,
and I will send punishment upon your daughters-in-law because
they commit adultery.
The men actually couple themselves with harlots
and they offer sacrifices with 'sacred' prostitutes.
A people without understanding will surely come to ruin.

5. The first two lines of verse 15 taken literalistically read:

¹⁵ If, Israel, you are a harlot...
Let not Judah be guilty.

However, the Hebrew 'If...' (*'im*) has another usage. It often indicates an oath formula, and comes to have the sense 'surely ...not'. When 'If' is part of an oath formula, it has the sense 'If this and that happens or is the case...let me come under the judgement of the oath'. This means that 'If...' has the sense of 'surely not'. In Psalm 95:11 'If they enter my rest' means 'They shall surely not enter my rest' and is rightly translated this way in the English translations (and in Hebrews 3:11!). The same idiomatic use of 'If' is found in Hosea 4:15. It should be translated:

¹⁵ Israel, you are surely not to be a harlot.
Let not Judah be guilty.

> **And do not come to Gilgal.**
> **And do not go up to Beth-Aven.**
> **And do not swear 'As Yahweh lives'.**

I did give a warning that the Hebrew text of Hosea is one of the more difficult parts of the Bible! Other parts of the Old Testament prophets are easier. Now we are ready to draw out the lessons of the text.

1. *One individual 'clergyman' may cause great damage to the church.*

First of all Hosea seems to address one particular person.

> **⁴ Surely God has a controversy with a certain person.**
> **And there is a person God reproves.**
> **With you surely is my controversy, O priest!**

It is quite possible that the priest whom God reproves is the same one who troubled Amos. Amos and Hosea were contemporaries and both of them ministered in the north. We know from Amos chapter 7 that there was a priest by the name of Amaziah who was much opposed to Amos. It is quite possible that he is the one referred to here. However this is not 100% certain, and it does not matter what the man's name was. It is enough to know that there was one particular high-priest who was a great enemy to God's message of righteousness. He had a colleague, a false-prophet who worked with him. And apparently the priest's mother also was an influential but evil woman. Often in the work of God a single opponent of God's kingdom arises to be a thorn in the flesh of the believing people of God.

2. *Those who damage God's church face severe warning.*

> **⁵ And you shall stumble in the day;**
> **and with you also the prophet shall stumble by night;**
> **and I shall destroy your mother.**

God issues a warning. The fact that a man has a title like 'priest' or 'prophet' will not save him. The exalted position of the mother in the family will not save her (cf. 10:14). The priest and his companion, the prophet (whoever they might be), will experience a serious downfall of some kind. The priest's mother will experience ruin. If any person destroys God's church, God will destroy him.

> **⁶ My people are destroyed for lack of knowledge
> because you have rejected knowledge.**

The reason why God was so angry was because of the bad influence the priest and his supporters had had in the northern territory of Israel. The priest had the task of teaching the Mosaic law and leading the people of God into righteousness. Although this man claimed to be a priest of Yahweh he was not providing the people with the knowledge that should come by his teaching of the law of God.

> **And I will reject you from being priest to me.
> You forgot the law of your God
> and I will forget your children – I on my part also.**

The 'children' could be family members of the priest or simply his priestly supporters. Verse 8 makes it clear that a small priestly group is still in mind. This priest apparently claimed to worship Yahweh yet encouraged pagan idolatry, in disregard of the law of Moses. God will 'forget' the priests children. That is, he will ostracize them, ignore their needs, snub their prayers, ignore their distresses.

3. *Hosea analyses their deterioration.*

> **⁷ As they became great, so they sinned against me.
> Their glory they changed into their shame.
> ⁸ They devour the sin-offering of my people,
> and towards their guilt-offering they lift up their appetite.**

Hosea maintains (i) that this priestly family is characterised by pride. 'Becoming great' seems to refer to rise in influence. But

increase in influence simply resulted in high-handed disobedience
to God.

They (ii) corrupted the worship of Israel. 'Their glory' was the
honour of priestly ministry for Yahweh. They turned it into 'shame',
the vile rites of pagan worship.

They (iii) were characterised by greed. The priests were allowed
to eat part of the offerings (Leviticus 6:17-23) but apparently were
greedy for more than their due share.

4. Soon God's judgement will fall.

> ⁹ **And it shall be 'Like people, like priest'.**
> **And I will visit upon him his ways;**
> **and his doings I shall return to him.**

The priests and the people affect each other. Leaders get the people
they deserve. People get the leaders they deserve. Only God's in-
tervening grace breaks the pattern. But as they are like each other
in spiritual decline, they shall be like each other in receiving judgement. The judgement of God is eventually a matter of exact retribution. Their 'ways' (persistent habits) and their 'deeds' (specific
actions) come back to receive just reprisal.

> ¹⁰ᵃ **They have eaten but will not be satisfied.**
> **They have been promiscuous but will not increase.**

Despite their greed for the meat of the sacrifices, their gluttony will
not be satisfied. Despite their harlotry, barrenness will characterise
their family.

It is sometimes helpful to invert biblical denunciations into
positive descriptions. If the priests of Hosea 4 are proud, corrupt,
forgetful of the law and greedy, what sort of leader is God looking
for? He is looking for humility, so that 'greatness' can come into a
person's life without its leading him into sinful carelessness. He is
looking for leaders who do not corrupt, but rather uphold, the
worship and service of God. He is looking for those who will

implement biblical standards, those who will be free from love of gain.

The priests of Hosea's times failed as teachers and encouraged national turning away from faith in Yahweh and loss of righteousness. They enticed the people into a mixture of paganism plus use of the name 'Yahweh'.

Christian leaders will earnestly give themselves to teaching the Word of God, will have an impact for righteousness throughout a nation, and will promote an undiluted faith in Yahweh.

Questions for Reflection

1. If parts of the Bible need expert handling, how does the ordinary Christian cope with reading the Bible?

2. Is it true today that one clergyman can do much damage to the church?

3. What sort of knowledge do Christians need so as not to be destroyed?

9. The Wind with its Wings (4:10b-19)

One key to understanding Hosea 4:4-19 is to note who the pronouns refer to. 'You' in 4:4, 5, 6, 13, 14 is the high-priest, the enemy of God's work. 'I' in 4:5, 6, 7, 8, 9, 12, 14 is God. 'They' in 4:7, 8, 10, 12, 13, 14 are the priest's supporters. 'He' in 4:9, 12 is the high-priest. In verse 15 'You' changes its meaning, but this is made clear by the phrase 'You, O Israel'. In verses 17, 18 'He' refers to God. 'They' continues to refer to the priestly party in northern Israel (4:18, 19). In verse 19, 'she' is an unnamed female goddess.

Firstly, *Hosea mentions the specific sins into which the priests have taken the people.*

> They have forsaken Yahweh to keep harlotry.
> [11] Harlotry, wine and new wine take away the heart [12] of my
> people.
> He makes enquiry from his wood; and his staff reports to him.
> For by a spirit of promiscuity he has led people astray.
> And they act promiscuously in defiance of their God.

(i) There was *harlotry* (4:10b). So powerful is the sexual urge within men and women that only the love of God or the most cruel and oppressive rules will restrain it from flowing into wrong channels of expression. The spiritual adultery of the nation led to quite literal immorality. The priestly families also were involved, although the law required that a daughter of a priest who engaged in such a lifestyle was to be burned by fire (Leviticus 21:9).

(ii) There was *drunkenness* (4:11). Although 'wine' was not forbidden in Israel, the combination of two words, 'wine (the common word) and sweet wine' (a more potent drink), suggests great excess. Although wine may 'gladden the heart of man' (Psalm 104:15), in Hosea's time it was 'taking away the heart', that is, depriving men and women of their judgement and self-control.

(iii) There was *'divination'* (4:12), rituals by which men try to get information concerning the unknown by contact with supernatural powers. 'He' – the high-priest – was seeking advice from his 'wood'. The priest's 'wood' or 'pole' was the 'Asherah', a wooden symbol of a female deity set up beside the altar. The high-priest was leading the people into occultism, defying God who had forbidden such symbolic poles (Deuteronomy 16:21). The modern pagan, likewise, turns aside from God and picks up the astrology charts to help him find his way. When people turn aside from God they still feel the need to get supernatural help and advice. Israel was to consult God when needing guidance concerning the future or the unknown.

(iv) There was *false worship* (4:13a).

> ¹³ Upon the mountaintops they offer sacrifices,
> and upon the hills they burn incense,
> under oak-trees, under poplars and under terebinths,
> because there the shade is good.

Verse 13 describes the rites and ceremonies of paganism in Israel. High-places on the tops of hills would be used for lascivious 'worship'. Large trees would be used as places of divination; the cool shade was regarded as useful for immoral purposes.

(v) There was *ruination of the family* (13b-14).

> Therefore your daughters are promiscuous,
> and your daughters-in-law commit adultery.
> ¹⁴ I will surely send punishment upon your daughters because
>   they are promiscuous,
> and I will send punishment upon your daughters-in-law because
>   they commit adultery.
> The men actually couple themselves with harlots
> and they offer sacrifices with 'sacred' prostitutes.
> A people without understanding will surely come to ruin.

The worship of the baals involved a kind of 'holy' immorality, in which lecherous reverence for the gods took place in the open-air sanctuaries on the hills; it symbolised and was thought to promote fertility. Family-relationships became unstable and incestuous. Since 'holy' prostitution was at the heart of the nation's worship it led to a culture in which relationships between the sexes were without purity, in which women who had been sex-objects even at sanctuaries continued to be viewed in such a way, and in which sexual liaisons were casual and unprincipled.

It all reflected deep ignorance of God and of the righteousness for which men and women were created. It would lead to the destruction of the society and the speedy end to the nation. 'A people without understanding will surely come to ruin'.

Secondly, *Hosea focuses on the areas of the land that have come under the influence of the decadent religion led by the priests.*

> [15] Israel, you are surely not to be a harlot.
> Let not Judah be guilty.
> And do not come to Gilgal.
> And do not go up to Beth-Aven.
> And do not swear 'As Yahweh lives'.

He looks at the different parts of the land: 'Israel ... Judah', and specific towns where there were sanctuaries, 'Gilgal ... Beth-Aven', as though he were roving around the country pointing to the places where idolatry and wickedness had got a grip. His thinking grasps hold of God's plans for the entire nation of Israel, Judah included.

'Israel' was the name given to Jacob after he 'wrestled with God' (Genesis 32:38). It became the name of a nation and reminded them of their origins. Their ancestor was one who was so eager for the blessing of God that he had held on to God in persistent faith until he received special blessing and an answer to his prayer.

'Judah' was, firstly, the name of the son of Jacob and Leah (Genesis 29:35). The name was linked with the Hebrew word for praise. It recalled Leah's remark, 'This time I will praise the Lord', and reminded the bearers of the name that they should be a people who praised.

'Gilgal' was near to the point where the Israelites had crossed the river Jordan a generation after their leaving Egypt. The name echoes the Hebrew word *galal*, 'to roll', for it was there that God had 'rolled away the disgrace of Egypt' from them (Joshua 5:9). The first passover took place there (Joshua 5:9, 10). A monument of twelve stones was set up there (Joshua 4:20) to remind the Israelites of how God had saved them, released them from bondage, given them victory over enemies, and given them a prosperous land, with promises of a great future. But now Gilgal was the centre of filthy 'worship' to gods who had never redeemed anyone!

'Beth-Aven' refers to Bethel. It was the place where Jacob's awareness of God was intensified. So real did God become to him,

he named the place 'Beth-El', 'house of God'. From that time on
Bethel was associated with meeting with God. Yet Hosea uses the
word 'Beth-Aven' ('house of iniquity'). He is playing with the word.

In Nairobi, where I live, the cost of living is high and there are
so many con-men walking the streets that we sometimes speak
about 'Nairobbery'. We are familiar with these kinds of playful
changes in names. Hosea is doing the same thing. Beth-El deserves
to be called Beth-Aven. It has become a house of iniquity. Jacob
the father of the nation called it 'House of God', and he called
Yahweh 'the God of Bethel' (Genesis 36:13; 35:7). But it was hardly
a 'House of God' in Hosea's time.

These names, Israel, Judah, Gilgal, and Bethel, should have
reminded any sensitive Israelite that God was the living God. The
people would even casually use the expression 'As Yahweh lives',
in taking oaths. Hosea says 'Don't do it'. The brusque commands
'You are not to be a harlot ... Let not Judah be guilty ... Don't come
to Gilgal ... Don't go up to Beth-Aven .... Don't say "As Yahweh
lives"' are as though he were saying, 'Don't use these place-names
that remind you that God is the living God. You have forgotten
everything about seeking God's blessing. You are not living for the
praise of Yahweh. You know nothing about disgrace rolling away
from you. You do not have the presence of God at all. And you
certainly know nothing of God as the living God.'

Thirdly, *Hosea protests against their stubbornness in sin.*

> ¹⁶ **For like a stubborn cow, Israel is being stubborn.**
> **Shall Yahweh now be shepherding them like a lamb in an open field?**
> ¹⁷ **Ephraim is joined to idols.**
> **He, for his part, has abandoned them.**
> ¹⁸ **He has turned aside from their drunkenness.**
> **They have practised harlotry.**
> **Their protectors have greatly loved dishonour.**

Israel is like a stubborn cow. How can Yahweh be a shepherd to
them? To be a shepherd requires sheep who are docile and ma-

noeuvrable. But they are not like sheep, they are like cows! God has abandoned them, for the moment, leaving them in their idolatry, turning with disgust from their drunkenness, hating their unchaste ways.

The rulers gave no lead. They were not ruling but rather following the mindless religiosity of Canaanite ways, greatly loving dishonour. The people and their female-idols are as good as swept away already. The Assyrians are knocking at the doors.

¹⁹ The wind with its wings has carried her away.
And they shall be ashamed because of their sacrifices.

Wind is often used of the blast of God's judgement (Psalms 1:4; 18:42; 35:5; 103:16) and the bible speaks of the 'wings of the wind' (see Psalm 18:10; 2 Samuel 22:11). The 'her' apparently refers to the leading goddess of the immoral cult.

Hosea 4:15-19 is a 'Liturgy of the Lost'[12], a lamentation over a society moving to its final catastrophe, after a long period of decay. Despite its wonderful origins, shared with Judah, in which Jacob met with God, there is no meeting with God now. Despite Yahweh's rolling disgrace away, they had turned to the 'freedom' of living without God. They had invented their own convenient religion which held out hopes of a cushy life and mixed in plenty of sex, but made no demands on the mind and certainly none on the will. It gave them a riot of 'worship' but required no discipline. It gave them the feeling that they were working with the magic of religion to get blessed by the gods. Immorality was institutionalised in Canaanite religion and now started in teenage years. It all seems rather familiar!

Hosea charges the national decadence to the priests, with a sideglance at the kings. The priests were meant to be the teachers of the law. Hosea himself is a prophet. He has only one weapon to use: the revelation he had received from God concerning the state of the nation.

---

12. J.L. Mays, *Hosea: A Commentary* (SCM, 1969), p.79.

An easy recovery for Israel will teach them nothing. They would only lapse back again in no time at all. Since 'Ephraim is joined to idols', God has abandoned them. Sometimes the way to rescue a nation is to abandon it. God vents his wrath and lets degradation prove the real nature of sin. Israel's immediate future was abandonment to the Assyrians. 'The wind with its wings' is about to blast the nation out of existence. It will be centuries before he will bring them back to himself and again be to them the God who had redeemed them by the blood of a lamb.

Questions for Reflection

1. Which of the sins that Hosea mentions are special weaknesses in our society?

2. Do specific geographical areas have particular proneness to sin?

3. Are today's leaders leaders or followers?

10. Unable to Turn to God (5:1-7)

There are many connections between 4:4-19 and 5:1-7; some commentators put the two sections within one unit. Yet the summons ('Hear this, O priests...') suggests that a sub-section starts here, and the further summons in 5:8 suggests that it ends at 5:7. Hosea has moved from the priests (in 4:4, 6, 9) to the people (4:12) and to the communities mentioned in 4:15, but the priests have not been forgotten.

> [1] Here this, O priests!
> And listen, O house of Israel!
> And, house of the king, give heed!
> Because this judgement is for you!
> For you have become a trap to Mizpah,
> and a snare spread out upon Tabor.

² Rebels have gone deep in depravity,
but I am a chastisement to them all.
³ I, yes I, know Ephraim,
and Israel is not hidden from me.
For, now, O Ephraim, you have been a harlot,
and Israel is defiled.
⁴ Their deeds will not permit them[13]
to turn to their God.
For a spirit of harlotry is among them,
and they do not know Yahweh.
⁵ Israel's pride will testify against it.
Both Israel and Ephraim will stumble in their iniquity
and Judah will stumble with them.
⁶ With their flocks and their herds
they will go to seek Yahweh,
but they will not find him.
He has withdrawn from them.
⁷ It is against Yahweh that they have been treacherous,
for they have fathered alien children.
Now he will consume[14] their portion at the new moon.

The main theme of the unit is the determination of God to be 'Chastisement' to the people. 'I am a chastisement', says God. The abstract noun almost makes it a title, 'I am Chastisement'[15].

1. *Great responsibility rests on those who claim to be leaders of God's people.* The unit calls upon 'the priests', the 'house of Israel' (which in this place is perhaps the ruling elite, as in 1:4) and the 'house of the king' (the officials at the king's palace); the decision about to be announced is specially for them (5:1). It is a great responsibility to be in any kind of leadership position. No one should

13. The 'm' at the beginning of *ma'alelehem* makes the 'm' ('them') at the end of *yitenu* unnecessary (for the 'm' can do double-duty). However no object is needed with Hebrew *natan* followed by an infinitive.
14. I take it that the 'm' at the end of *yo'kelem* ('consume') is not a suffix ('them') but is the Hebrew 'enclitic mem' adding emphasis.
15. See Andersen, *Hosea*, p.388.

lightly take such honour upon himself (see Hebrews 5:4). Not many should be teachers (James 3:1); they will face a severer judgement.

The leaders of the land have become 'a trap ... a snare'. Mizpah was probably the southern town where Samuel gathered the Israelites to renew the nation in the ways of obedience (see 1 Samuel 7:5-12, 16); it had been a centre of spiritual renewal. Now, under the leaders of the nation, it has become a place of deceit. The people, instead of being led in the ways of righteousness, are brought into pathways of idolatry. Tabor was a mountain further north, about 19 kilometres south-west of the Sea of Galilee. It has a flat top, so it was suitable as a site for idolatrous ceremonies.

2. *Entanglement in sin can be so severe that it leads to spiritual enslavement.* Hosea emphasizes their being enmeshed in the trap and snare of sinful ways. There are degrees of entanglement in sin. It is possible to be overcome to a lesser or greater extent.

God sometimes seems to do nothing at all about sin. The woman caught in adultery was told 'Go and sin no more' and seems to have faced no further consequence for what she had done. Sometimes God will say 'The Lord has put away your sin' (2 Samuel 12:13) but will go on to speak of accompanying disciplines ('However...', 2 Samuel 12:14).

Here in Hosea 5 we have an entanglement in sin and depravity which goes further than any of this. It was two hundred years old. It had involved at least one serious decline and partial restoration. The nation had sunk to a low level in the days of Ahab and Jezebel in the 9th century but God had sent Elijah and Elisha to rescue them. He had arranged for Hazael to distress them and for Jehu to violently purge the nation of Ahab's cult (1 Kings 19:17). Despite Jehu's harshness (which in Hosea 1:4 itself received condemnation) the opening events of his reign had provided an opportunity for change; Ahab's idolatry had been savagely exterminated.

Yet the nation had still persisted in idolatry. Now it seems that they are sinking as low as they had gone in the days of Ahab. 'The rebels have gone deep in depravity' (5:2). Idolatry and its immoralities had become so ingrained and habitual that there was no likelihood of their amending their ways. 'Their deeds will not permit them to turn to their God.'

Hosea attributes it to a 'spirit', not an 'evil spirit' as that term is used in the gospels, but an ingrained and powerful ethos of immorality which had got hold of the people of Israel.

3. *God had, for the moment, withdrawn the possibility of repentance.* God says, 'I am a chastisement to them all'. He is about to plunge the nation into a severe chastisement that will last for centuries. Only a few individual believers will remain. God has taken note of what is happening in Ephraim, and how the nation has turned to 'lovers' in the form of the baals. The nation has been seriously defiled and God's action will be severe (5:3).

Hosea 5:4 reminds us of Hebrews 6:3-6, except that Hosea deals with the history of a nation. It is always easier not to sin in the first place than to sin and repent later, for one may not be able to repent! God might not give the ability to repent (Hebrews 6:3)! Repentance requires heeding God's voice. If one becomes 'stone deaf to the Spirit'[16] it is impossible to be renewed to repentance. In Hosea 5:4 a *nation* is not hearing God's voice. There were exceptions (otherwise Hosea would not be saying anything; there is no point in speaking to those who are stone deaf) but on the whole the nation is beyond repentance. Sin has set up a total slavery. They do not know God. So deaf are they to the pleas of God, they walk around in proud self-confidence. 'Israel's pride will testify against it' (5:5).

The chastisement takes the form of God's withdrawal. Israel's sin will lead to a serious fall; the Assyrians will soon be arriving. Then something similar will happen to the Judeans also; in their case the Babylonians will prove to be the agent of chastisement.

At such a time they might seek God, but it will be too late to

16. See R.T. Kendall, *Stone Deaf To the Spirit or Rediscovering God* (Christian Focus, 1994).

bring about a change. No response will come from God. They have reached a point where at that precise moment there is no remedy. They will later be invited to return to God (14:1-9), but at this point they are not even called to repentance. On the contrary, if they do seek God, he will take no notice. 'With their flocks and their herds (plenty of animals to sacrifice!) they will go to seek Yahweh, but they will not find him. He has withdrawn from them' (5:6).

A person or a nation undergoing advanced chastening is at the mercy of God's timing. Not even repentance will necessarily lead to immediate restoration. Any hope of restoration is found not in an immediate avoiding of chastening but rather in the discipline of going through chastening.

Hosea calls upon those who might listen – and they would be few – to accept God's verdict and submit to it. They must look to a future undated occasion when God would have mercy on Israel again. Individuals taking notice of Hosea may themselves be aware of God and in fellowship with him, but the nation has a grim future. It is perilously close to destruction at the hands of the Assyrians. Perhaps they will be so alarmed at Hosea's words that these will have a good effect after all! But Hosea had no easy answers.

In point of historical fact, Israel did not recover at this point. The Assyrians arrived; Israel lost its identity and became an Assyrian province. Only in the gospel of Jesus would there come some measure of restoration for 'Samaria' (as it would be called) and a greater measure of restoration for Israel is still in the future.

The seriousness of their sin is seen in (i) whom it is against ('It is against Yahweh that they have been treacherous'), (ii) the results it has brought ('they have fathered alien children') and (iii) the consequence it brings ('God will consume their portion at the new moon'). 'Portion' is a word which has to do with inheritance. The 'new moon' was a religious festival. At the beginning of each lunar month there would be a time of religious ritual. The closing word of this unit is that at the point where the Israelites are indulging in their Canaanite 'religious immorality' God will take action. Their inheritance will be lost. In Israel 'inheritance' was largely a matter of land. Their land will be taken away because they will be taken away from their land. God's relationship with northern Israel will come to a standstill.

Was there any hope at all? Yes, in two ways. Those who heeded Hosea's message would in their own lives be exempt. In their own relationship with God, they would know his salvation. Though a community may have 'lost its first love', the invitation remains open 'if any *one* person hears my voice, I shall open the door and will eat a meal with him, and he – that individual – will enjoy a meal with me' (see Revelation 3:20).

Also the story of Israel was not totally finished. Death might seem to be the end, and Hosea is predicting the death of the nation. But God is a God of resurrection! And it is 'resurrection' from spiritual death that Hosea looks for (6:2). There is no 'oath' mentioned here after which God will not change his mind. Perhaps they will repent after all. As the king of Nineveh would have said: 'Let people call on God ... Who knows? God may turn and relent, and withdraw his burning anger so that we shall not perish' (Jonah 3:9). The people who first read Hebrews 6:3-6 had *not* gone beyond recall. 'Though we are speaking in this way ... we are convinced of better things ...' (Hebrews 6:9). Victory might be snatched from the jaws of defeat. People who are not stone deaf to the Spirit might rediscover God.

Questions for Reflection

1. What do you think about the thought of God's withdrawing from people?

2. Are we dependent on Christian leaders for the well-being of the churches?

3. Can a Christian be entangled in sin?

11. Sound an Alarm! (5:8-12)

So far in the book of Hosea the background has been the affluent and indulgent reign of Jeroboam II (782/1-753). Hosea chapters 1-3 spoke of the end of the house of Jehu, which had five kings (Jehu, Jehoahaz, Joash, Jeroboam II, Zechariah). Shortly after the end of Jeroboam's reign (753/752) *Zechariah* was murdered, and a new dynasty began (see 2 Kings 15:8-12).

The background of Hosea 5:8-7:16 is somewhat later. The clue is in 5:13 where Israel sends to Assyria for help. We know that Ahaz of Judah did this in about 732, to get help *against* Israel, but when did Israel ask for help? The allusion must be to the time around 744 when Tiglath-Pileser ('Pul') had just become king, and Menahem made a payment for Assyria's patronage (see 2 Kings 15:19-20).

We must keep in mind the sequence of the various kings of Israel.

Jeroboam II	782/1-753
Zechariah	753-752
Shallum	752
Menahem	752-742/1
Pekahiah	742/1-740/39
Pekah	740/39-732/1
Hoshea	732/1-723

When Assyria invaded Israel, Menahem paid a large sum to have Assyria as an ally rather than as an enemy. Something similar happened years later in about 732 when Hoshea of Israel, having assassinated Pekah, appealed to Assyria for peace and made payment for the protection of Assyria (see 2 Kings 17:3). Some commentators think Hosea 5:8-7:16 dates from the later payment and alludes to the Syro-Ephraimite alliance and invasion of Judah in about 735. Yet 2 Kings 17:4 refers to Hoshea's appealing to Egypt against Assyria, whereas Hosea 5:13 refers to an appeal to Assyria against unmentioned enemies. Although Israel no doubt appealed to both countries (7:11, 'they call to Egypt, they go to Assyria') they probably did not do so at the same time, and 2 Kings 17:4 mentions only Egypt. It is more likely that the background is in the time of Menahem (752-742/1). Hosea 5:8-7:16 gives the impression of being Hosea's warnings, at some time *before* the events, about what was about to happen.

The Syro-Ephraimite alliance and invasion of Judah in about 740-735 is the fulfilment of Hosea's predictions, not its background. Douglas Stuart who thinks the Syro-Ephraimite war is alluded to here has to ask the question, 'Why, then, does God speak of a future judgement ... if the invasion is over?' and then he finds the fulfilment of the warnings in the events of 722 and beyond.[17] I judge that the *setting* is earlier, in the days of Menahem, and the *fulfilment* includes all the events of the Syro-Ephraimite war and much more, ending in the fall of Jerusalem in 587.

What happened was this. The murderer of Zechariah was *Shallum*, but he was himself killed within a month (2 Kings 15:13-16). The next reign of any length was that of *Menahem*. His line lasted a little longer. He himself reigned about ten years (752-742/1; see 2 Kings 15:17-22) and was succeeded by his son *Pekahiah* (742/1-740) who was duly assassinated by one of his officers *Pekah* (see 2 Kings 15:23-26).

During this time the Assyrian menace grew. A series of Assyrian kings was becoming powerful. It began in the days of *Ashurnasirpal II* (885-860) who had expanded his realm to the west in the direction of Israel. *Shalmanesar III* (859-824) enlarged the kingdom yet further. At the battle at Qarqar in 853, Ahab of Israel had joined with other nations in trying to resist Assyria. We know also from Assyrian records that Jehu of Israel paid taxes to Shalmanesar. *Shamshi-Adad V* (823-810) followed, then *Adad-nirari* (810-783/2), then *Shalmanesar IV* (783/2-773/2). Could Jeroboam not see that Assyria was getting nearer?

Shalmanesar IV put a lot of pressure on the Arameans in

---

17. D. Stuart, *Hosea-Jonah* (WBC, Word, 1987), p.102.

Damascus and it was probably this that allowed Jeroboam to expand his border northward towards Aram (2 Kings 14:25). But if the kingdom of Damascus was about to fall to the Assyrians, might Israel not be the next kingdom to fall? To live in rebellion against God is to live on the edge of a volcano.

The growth of Assyrian power continued during the reign of Jeroboam. In the second half of his reign his Assyrian counterpart was *Ashur-Dan III* (772/1-755/4). In his days Jonah was sent to the capital city Nineveh (Jonah 1:1), maybe at some time after 760.

After the time of Jeroboam II came *Ashur-nirari V* (754/3-746/5) and *Tiglath-Pileser III,* also called 'Pul' (745/4-727/6).

Tiglath-Pileser III began to put serious pressure on Israel. During Menahem's rule, he marched into the Palestinian area and brought the kingdom of Damascus to an end. Menahem was forced to surrender Israel's independence, and to pay a heavy tax to Assyria 'that Pul might help him to establish his grip on royal power' (2 Kings 15:19). This caused resentment among the people. After Menahem had died (742/1) and after Pekahiah his son had reigned for two years, the next king, Pekah of Israel, joined forces with Rezin of Damascus in an invasion of Judah (the 'Syro-Ephraimite war' as it is called). Their idea was to force Judah to join in a triple alliance against Assyria.

In 732/1 Tiglath-Pileser removed Pekah and put Hoshea on the throne. When Tiglath-Pileser died in 727 Hoshea tried to throw off the domination of Assyria. He refused to give tribute to Shalmanesar V and sent to Egypt for help. But Egypt sent no help. Samaria was overcome and the city's population was deported by the next Assyrian king, Sargon II. Sargon II (722/1-705/4) initiated a scheme of mass deportation. The nation of northern Israel ceased to exist. Jeroboam had been sitting on the edge of a volcano. Repentance would have brought a turn-about, but to continue in the ways of idolatry was fatal. Throughout the long days of Jeroboam the LORD was giving them a last chance. The nation had one generation left before the volcano would erupt.

It is the early stages of this increasingly threatening situation

which is the background to Hosea's warning. It must come from
the time of Menahem and refer to the period when he paid a bribe
to secure Assyria's help. Our concern in all this, however, is to see
the message of Hosea. Hosea writes before the events and sees an
enemy who is about to come to devastate the land. Israel's sin is
causing God to bring an enemy nearer and nearer. In his mercy the
nation is getting a warning through Hosea.

> **8 Blow the horn in Gibeah**
> **and blow the trumpet in Ramah.**
> **Sound an alarm in Beth-Aven.**
> **Look behind you, Benjamin.**

1. *To receive a warning is a great privilege.* Sin is being committed all over Israel, so God wants a warning to be sounded throughout the land. Verse 8 refers to battle-alarms and calls to war. Gibeah
and Ramah were hilltop towns a few miles north of Jerusalem.
They were places from which one might first see in the distance an
invading army. They were areas near the border of Judah. The
Assyrians were a threat to both Israel and Judah.

Why are warnings given? They are given because otherwise
the people would be unaware of what was happening. Warning is
an essential ingredient in preaching. People just tend to go on their
way 'eating ... drinking ... marrying ... giving in marriage', con-
tinuing the normal round of life with its pleasures and pursuits. Yet
while that is happening, sin is getting worse. Society does not evolve
into godliness; rather it declines into wickedness. It needs warnings.
Also the process of decay is slow. Israel had been in existence for
almost two hundred years. The people were assuming that things
would go on the way they had for ever. We can never quite believe
that calamity will come our way. 'It will never happen to us', is the
feeling we have in our hearts. Hosea says 'Not so!' Blow the horn!
Sound the alarm!

2. *God's warnings include predictions.* Hosea gives a specific prediction of what God's judgement will be. Without mentioning the

name of the invader, Hosea predicts incisively that devastating invasion will soon occur.

> ⁹**Ephraim shall be desolate in the day of rebuke.**
> **Among the tribes of Israel I am making it known with certainty.**

The prophets of Israel often gave direct predictions as warnings and encouragements to their hearers and readers. Almost every true prophet of Israel was a foreteller of the future. It was not simply that they were guessing. They had 'stood in the counsel of the LORD' (see Jeremiah 23:22) and often gave quite exact statements about what was to happen. They were not following hopeful impulses. Rather they were conscious that God had spoken to them and they were 'making it known with certainty'.

In varying degrees Christian prophecy still fulfils this function. It is to be tested. It cannot give new doctrines. It rarely has the precision or accuracy of the biblical writers, but it is still true that our lives in the present are moulded by warnings and predictions concerning the future. God is still a God who speaks. The foundational doctrines of the Christian faith are given to us and cannot be increased until Jesus comes. The greatest prediction that moulds our hopes and our thinking concerns the second coming of Jesus. Yet even lesser events can be revealed in advance, and if due caution is exercised and we resist the wild predictions of eccentrics, then we still live in the present, in the light of our knowledge of what is to come.

3. *Hosea focuses on the essence of Israel's sin*: rejection of God's guidelines (5:10).

> ¹⁰ **The princes of Judah are like**
> **those who remove landmarks.**

The reference is to the regulation in the Mosaic law that those who move their neighbour's boundary marks are under a curse (Deuteronomy 19:14; 27:17). The regulation is used as a parable. The civic leaders of Israel have 'moved landmarks' in their idolatry, their encouragement of violence, their immorality.

4. *Hosea announces God's imminent wrath.* They have had warning for many years. Now they are at the very last stages of the existence of the nation.

> I will pour out my wrath upon them like a flood of water.
> ¹¹ Ephraim is oppressed, crushed in judgement,
> because he willingly walked after emptiness.
> ¹² So I am like decay to Ephraim
> and like rottenness to the house of Judah.

The judgement of God is like sickness. The Hebrew words for 'decay' and 'rottenness' are difficult to translate with certainty, and yet it is clear that they refer to deterioration of health. Israel is like a nation whose health is steadily declining under the judgement of God. Soon the nation will be no more. The process is slow; God is like an agent of decay. But soon the end will come and then God will be like a lion (5:14)!

The nation is being given very last opportunities. The way of spiritual recovery is not *totally* closed for Israel; the people might after all rediscover God. God is still speaking to them. 'Blow the horn ... blow the trumpet ... Sound an alarm ...'.

Questions for Reflection

1. How can we warn the world without seeming morbid and negative?

2. To what extent can we be forewarned about future events?

3. What today are the landmarks that should never be moved?

12. Turning to a Mistaken Remedy (5:13-15)

The plight of Israel was so desperate that at one point they began to
see it for themselves.

In the days of Jeroboam II the people had been complacent.
Then Jeroboam's reign finished. Two years later the house of Jehu
was brought to an end altogether. The political situation was unstable. Assyria was growing in power and aggression. Israel's years
of injustice, immorality, violence and corruption of every kind
had not prepared them for these days of danger.

To make matters worse they turn to wrong solutions. Instead of
sensing that God is dealing with them, they think the answer is to be
found in the realm of international politics.

1. *There was a partial recognition of need.* The swing of events
since the death of Jeroboam has alarmed the people. Two kings
had been killed in recent years. Menahem was unpopular. The
Assyrians were menacing. Tiglath-Pileser is on the throne. In Judah
the affluent reign of Azariah (also called Uzziah) will soon end, and
Judah feels threatened as well as Israel.

Suddenly both nations, Israel and Judah, become aware that
their society is facing crisis and that they are in no state to survive
the future.

Sometimes it happens that people live lives of carelessness, in
disregard of God's 'boundary stones', and then suddenly crisis brings
them up sharp. It may be political crisis within their country that
seems as if it will soon shatter all their prosperity. It might be that
they commit some sin they never thought they would commit. It
may be that the country's politics become so disgraceful that all
hope is lost in the political process altogether. It may be some kind
of 'mid-life crisis' in which a man suddenly realises that that for
which he has been living and hoping is never to be fulfilled, and he
wonders what he is actually living for anyway. Then he sees that he
himself is not right at heart.

It happened in Israel and Judah at about the same time.

**¹³ Ephraim saw his sickness,
and Judah saw his wound.**

Abruptly both nations became aware of their need.

2. *There was a mistaken turning to a useless remedy.* Although
Hosea keeps involving Judah in what he says, his main audience is
in Israel.

> **So Ephraim went to Assyria;
> he sent to the great king[18].**

When we suddenly see our need, our next danger is that we turn in
the wrong direction It happened repeatedly in the stories of Israel
and Judah. Ahaz of Judah did the same thing some years later.
When he was turning to Assyria, Isaiah would say to him: 'If you
will not believe, surely you will not be established' (Isaiah 7:9).

People's faith in men and women is so much greater than their
faith in God. Israel is happy to turn to Assyria which is nothing
more than a cruel and oppressive colonising power. Yet the people
will not turn to Yahweh who years before had rescued them from
oppression and was famous for delivering his people from crisis
after crisis. So today, people turn to pleasures, money, sexuality
and affluence, and then suddenly their gods let them down, and
then they think the answer is in economics or in a new political
party – or whatever. They forsake 'the fountain of living waters' to
turn to 'broken cisterns, that can hold no water' (Jeremiah 2:13).

The mistake consisted in Israel's thinking that it was its *situation* that needed help. The nation was surrounded by enemies. 'We
need a great king to be on our side', they felt. It was the same
problem that had been there right at the beginning of the Israelite
kingdom. 'We will have a king ... to fight our battles' (1 Samuel
8:20). They felt that they *themselves* were basically alright. They

---

18. The Hebrew says *mlk yrb* ('a king who will contend' or 'King Yareb').
More likely it should be read as *mlky rb*, ('the great king') which is a
common title for senior kings who were overlords of junior kings.

simply needed a great king to ensure their safety in a threatening world. It did not occur to them that their problem was not their situation but themselves! We are our own biggest problem. Assyria would not be the answer. They needed, not Assyria, but God's favour. As Isaiah would put it in a later Assyrian crisis, 'The people did not turn to him who smote them, nor seek Yahweh the omnipotent' (Isaiah 9:13).

3. *Their remedy would inevitably fail.* There was no help to be found in any king of Assyria. He was not the answer. He was one of their problems. To walk into the arms of the king of Assyria would be like a mouse looking to a cat for protection. Hosea says

> **But he is not able to heal you,**
> **and he will not cure you of your wound.**

Sinners can be strangely optimistic and short-sighted when they are in trouble. Did they really think that Assyria was the answer to their needs? Assyria was not looking upon Israel with any tenderheartedness. Assyria did not have the sympathy, nor the ability. 'He is not able to heal you'. Israel's problem was that of being in the grip of centuries of idolatrous and wicked ways. Assyria could not deal with that! Assyria had no intention of being fatherly to Israel. He might present himself as a kind of fatherly protector and patron of little nations like Israel, but the fatherly protector would soon turn out to be 'the rod of God's anger', 'a godless nation', one 'whose idols were greater than those of Jerusalem'. Isaiah would speak about God's punishing 'the arrogant boasting of the king of Assyria' (Isaiah 10:5, 6, 10, 12).

4. *God lets them know the true situation.*
They thought their problems lay in the enemies around them, but Hosea reveals to them, in the name of God, that it is God himself who is their problem!

> [14] **For I will be like a lion to Ephraim,**
> **and like a young lion to the house of Judah.**

It is not simply that Assyria or Egypt or some nearby nation is threatening them. Their deeper quandary is that God himself is roaring against them like a lion about to spring on its prey.

Hosea is known as the 'prophet of love'. Yet he lets us know that God can be angry or wrathful. God's love is not complacent about sin.

It is not that the wrath of God and the love of God are exactly parallel. The Bible never says 'God is wrath' in the way that it can say that 'God is love'. The Bible never says 'God *began* to love'; it does say 'God *became* angry'. God's anger is always a *re*-action. God's love wells up within himself.

But God can be like a roaring lion. He is about to bring suffering, destruction and ruin upon the land of Israel. To be hastening to Assyria is not the answer when God is determined to bring Israel to face the consequences of many years of accumulated rebellion.

The wrath of God is not God's losing his temper. There is no loss of control when God is angry (as in human anger, generally). It is never an 'explosion'; it is never unpredictable; it is never without warning. It is one of God's perfections.

It is roused by rejection of love. It is roused by sin, especially the sin of idolatry (see Deuteronomy 6:14ff.; Joshua 23:16).

God's anger is his purposeful reaction to sin and evil, by means of which he wishes to express his revulsion and call people to repentance. 'Let me alone', says God, '... that my wrath may burn hot...' (Exodus 32:10). God's anger is purposeful; it is a decision.

God's anger is a *re-action*. It is not inherent and spontaneous, as is his love. Love in God is eternal. But wrath does not belong to his very being in the way that love does. His wrath is never spontaneous. He *becomes* angry; he *is* love. God's anger is holy anger. It burns when his holiness and his righteous ways are scorned. God's anger is injured love. We remember Hosea's marriage. Hosea could take very strong action against his wife. But it was holy anger,

loving anger, the anger that arises as a consequence of unfaithfulness. It is only when we resist God's love that God's anger becomes final, and destructive and disastrous for us.

This was Israel's problem. Not Assyria, not Egypt, not its inter-
nal chaos. Those matters were simply the symptoms of a deeper
sickness, alienation from God. God was displeased with them.

5. *There was a doorway left open for treatment.*

> **¹⁵ I will go away and return to my place,
> until they acknowledge their guilt,
> and seek my face.
> In their trouble they will seek me earnestly.**

God plans to leave them until a change of heart takes place. Just as
Hosea said to his wife 'For many days you will wait for me' (3:3),
so God says to Israel that 'during many days the Israelites will wait
... Afterwards, the Israelites will return' (3:4, 5).

The anger of God can be halted (see Psalm 78:38; Amos 7:2ff.;
Hosea 11:8-9), but they must first acknowledge their guilt. They
must get to the point where they realise that it is their sin that has
brought many national crises upon the land.

Then they must seek God. They have been seeking Assyria.
Now let them seek God. God is waiting for the repentance of his
people. The experience of God's wrath is not the last word. 'His
place' is his heavenly home. He will withdraw to his place for a
while, leaving Israel without the manifestation of his presence. He
will leave them to face the devastating events that lay ahead of
them.

At times suffering has a strange power to make us face ourselves. True, it can arouse intense bitterness, but it can lead in
another direction also. God predicts that he will let so many troubles come upon Israel over the course of many years, that it will
eventually lead his people to see that they need the God of Israel to
help them. They will, says Hosea, turn and find a refuge in God.

Questions for Reflection

1. Is there any sign of our society seeing its need?

2. What are the useless remedies one turn to today?

3. Can God be our enemy?

13. Returning to the Lord (6:1-3)

Hosea 6:1-3 picks up on the last thought of Hosea 5:13-15. The only hope for Israel is to turn to God. Earlier in the prophecy, Hosea described the people as unable to turn to God. 'Their deeds will not permit them to turn to their God' (5:4). Yet this is not the last word on the subject. There will be some among the people of Israel who are willing to seek God. God always leaves a remnant. And the time may come when Yahweh will work among his people again. Hosea has hopes that spiritual awakening will come. Although Israel has sunk deeply in sin, Hosea has not given up on her. His great love for his wife led him to persist in striving to hold her affections, no matter what she did. He had spent years of his life trying to retain Gomer's affection and get loving responsiveness from her. God is like that too! God is persisting with Israel no matter how deeply entrenched in sin she may be. So the prediction in Hosea 5:15 is transposed into an plea in 6:1-3.

> [1] Come, let us return to Yahweh,
> for he has torn us, but he will heal is.
> He has wounded us, but he will bandage us.
> [2] He will revive us after two days,
> he will raise us up on the third day,
> and we shall live before him.
> [3] So let us get to know Yahweh,
> let us follow after knowing Yahweh.
> His appearance is as certain as sunrise
> and he will come to us like the rain,
> like the spring rain coming down upon the earth.

1. *First, he makes an appeal:* 'Come, let us return to Yahweh...'.
He uses the name 'Yahweh', the Exodus-name of the God who
redeems by the blood of a lamb. They are not returning to an unknown God, or to a philosophical idea. Rather they are turning to
one who is well-known to them in their history. 'Yahweh' was the
God who 'got himself a name' when he saved Israel from bondage,
releasing them by blood-atonement. This God has proved himself
to them before. All their idols have proved themselves to be failures. Why should they not turn back to one who has always proved
himself to be sheer goodness and kindness. Why should they not
abandon their lovers and turn to the great Lover of all? Hosea's
marriage is in the background of the thought – as it is throughout
the book. Why should the enslaved wife not come back to one who
has always been kindly, considerate and tender?

It is not a return to religiosity that Hosea wants. There was
plenty of religious routine in their lives already. They went to meetings, and had some kind of 'worship' on the top of hills. They
already went on pilgrimages to Gilgal and Bethel. They had plenty
of religious routine! Hosea invites them instead to turn to God! It
is possible to have what one can call 'religiosity' in one's life –
even Christian religiosity or evangelical religiosity or penetecostal
religiosity – without having God!

Turning to God is something that they themselves must do. They
might be happy to pray for Yahweh's blessing, but Yahweh has
withdrawn from them. A few prayers for help will do no good. On
their side there must be a turning to God. Hosea is speaking of God
in a very human way (something we are allowed to do). He pictures
God as having withdrawn to his heavenly home. There will be no
blessing for northern Israel any more – until they turn to him.

Turning to God will involve amendment of life. It is worth not-
ing the precise meanings of some Hebrew verbs at this point. The
Hebrew verb 'turn' (*shub*) is used here. There is a difference in the
Hebrew Old Testament between the Hebrew verb *nicham* which
means 'grieve', 'feel displeasure', 'regret' and the Hebrew word
shub, which means 'turn', 'return', 'revert'. Both words are some-

times translated 'repent' yet there is an important difference between the two. The first stresses feelings; the other stresses direction. The difference is important theologically (one is part of faith; the other follows faith)[19]. Occasionally the two verbs come in one sentence. I Kings 8:47,48 says that if the people of Israel sin but then 'take thought ... regret ... return ...', God will restore them. The verse mentions the mind ('take thought'), and the feelings ('regret') and then action ('return'). The word here in Hosea 6 focuses on the final action.

2. *He asks them to recognize the chastening of God.* The chastening of God has no value if there is no realisation of what is happening. Sheer suffering in and of itself simply produces bitterness and despair. Hosea invites the Israelites to see a purpose in what has happened to them. 'He has torn us ... He has wounded us'. They are to see the hand of God in the devastations that have come. They are experiencing military threats. The economy has declined since the days of Jeroboam II. Their immoralities have destroyed family life. They have brought the consequences of sin upon themselves. And yet God has had a hand in it too. 'He has torn us ... He has wounded us'.

3. *He invites them to trust in God's goodness.* Though God has torn them, and wounded them, Hosea does not believe that the wrath of God is his final word in this situation. If Hosea had believed that God's wrath was utterly final at this point he would not be ministering

---

19. See Calvin, *Institutes*, III, 3, 1, 5, where Calvin says repentance follows faith and is 'through' faith. In III, 3,5 he explicitly makes the point that it is *shub* he has in mind. We may notice the difference in the New Testament between *metanoieo*, 'change your mind', 'rethink', 'repent', and *epistrepho*, 'turn'. One is the first breath of faith ('Repent ... believe', Mark 1:15) The other is the amendment of life which is the subsequent development of faith ('Repent therefore and turn', Acts 3:19; 'repent and turn', Acts 26:20). Calvin knew what he was doing when he put repentance after faith. The practical aspects of this are set out in John Colquhoun's *Repentance* (Banner of Truth, 1965).

to them at all. Yet Hosea knows that God's chastenings are preliminary to his restorations. 'He will heal us ... He will bandage us'.

4. *Hosea asks them to believe that God's delay will not be unbear-
able.* Many Israelites might be tempted to believe that after such
deep sinfulness God would be likely to hold the nation in suffering
for a long time. The timing of God's chastening is in his hands. No
one can release themselves from God's disciplinary rebukes.
'Surely God will keep us in suffering for a long time', they might
feel. 'Not so!' says Hosea. The interval between repentance and
renewal of the nation will not be intolerable.

> [2] **He will revive us after a couple of days,**
> **he will raise us up on the third day.**

The phrase 'after a couple of days' probably denotes a short time.
'On the third day', as well as being a piece of common Canaanite
literary style (using an 'n, n + 1' increase of numbers as in Ecclesiastes 11:2 and elsewhere), also denotes a short period. If they will
turn to God, their resurrection from spiritual death will not take as
long as they might think.

The fact that Hosea uses the language of resurrection shows us
how serious the situation was in Israel. Although Hosea can use
the language of sickness ('torn ... heal ... wounded ... bandage') he
can also use the language of death. One could say that Israel needs
healing; one could equally say that Israel needs resurrection. It needs
quickening from its 'death-like state of rejection from the face of
God'.[20]

5. *Hosea promises that repentance will lead to renewal of life.* He
has confidence about the results of seeking God. They will be revived...

> **... and we shall live before him.**

---

20. F.D. Keil, *The Twelve Minor Prophets* (ET Eerdmans, 1949), p.96.

The central blessing of salvation is *life*. The gospels call it 'eternal life' but from the earliest parts of the biblical revelation God's gift to mankind has been called 'life'. In paradise there was an offer of 'life' (Genesis 2:9); it was life that man lost by disobedience (Genesis 3:22). A return to God, Hosea promises, will lead to renewed liveliness in obedience, in being a light to the nations. Life in the presence of God is the greatest blessing known. The New Testament simply develops an old theme: Jesus spoke of 'a well of water springing up into eternal life' (John 4:14).

In verse 3 Hosea renews his appeal, using different words.

> ³ **So let us get to know Yahweh,**
> **let us follow after knowing Yahweh.**

He has said 'Let us return'. Now he says 'Let us ... get to know, let us follow on to know ...'. God may be known! Both at a national level and at a personal level there is such a thing as being acquainted with God as a person, as a friend and guide. Israel has lapsed into chaos because the nation has ceased to be aware of God as a living reality in its life. Now Hosea asks them to pursue that knowledge of God once again.

In using the word 'follow on' or 'pursue', Hosea lets us know that this seeking of God will require persistence. They had 'pursued' their lovers (2:7); now let them spend an equal or greater energy in seeking God. Otherwise, if Israel throws aside what is good, an enemy will pursue the nation (8:3). To seek God will require more than a casual promise, more than a flash of half-hearted regrets. It will require persistence and determination.

If they will seek God in this way, God will be found by them. Hosea renews the promise that God will certainly respond.

> **His appearance is as certain as sunrise.**
> **And he will come to us like the rain,**
> **like the spring rain coming down upon the earth.**

Earlier, Hosea had referred to God's departure (5:15). Now he speaks of God's return. He will come like the warmth of the sun. He will come like the refreshment of rains in a hot country. A new season will come into their lives. It will be like sunrise. It will be like the freshness of spring rains.

Many of us need Hosea's call. The Christian life never stands stationary. It grows and flourishes or it decays and wilts. Often we stand in need of a new touch from God. Hosea's promise to Israel can be simply taken as for ourselves.

> 'If we ask you will come
> Send your rain on everyone
> ...For every child needs rain, spring rain'[21]

Questions for Reflection

1. Do God's people lose the ability to turn to God?

2. What does it mean to turn to God?

3. Does it matter whether full repentance is before or after faith?

14. Love Like the Morning Mist (6:4-6)
The sections of Hosea in 5:8 to 6:6 began with a trumpet-blowing alarm about the sin of Israel (5:8-9), in which Judah also is involved (5:10). Judgement, said Hosea, was about to fall on both (5:11). The two countries must not turn to mistaken remedies (5:13-15); instead Hosea calls them to repentance (6:1-3), and in the name of God expresses concern that their zeal for God is at the present a feeble matter (6:4-6). There is steady logical progress in these units.

At the time in which Hosea lived, Israel and Judah were very far from repentant. God is amazed at the behaviour of Israel and Judah (6:4a); their love towards him is volatile (6:4b). Yet God has done

---

21. A song sung by Kevin Prosch (see 'Come to the Light', Cassette Tape, Kingsway Music, KMC 679, UK).

so much in sending his word to them (6:5). What he is looking for in his people is mercy and the knowledge of God.

Let us dwell briefly on each of these points.

1. *The patient love of God.* Hosea uses very human language about God. If man is made in the image of God it means that God is human-like as well as that man is God-like. There is something in the heart of God that corresponds to our horror and amazement at unexpectedly bad treatment.

So God says:

> 4 What shall I do with you, O Ephraim?
> What shall I do with you, O Judah?

Again, Hosea's marriage is in the background here. Hosea had treated his wife well, and had shown her much love and affection. Hosea was amazed that someone could sink as low as Gomer had. At points he must have been in despair and must have uttered words very similar to these. 'What shall I do with you, Gomer?' He must have been in great agony when he could not stop his wife going after her lovers. God feels the same way about his people when they wander, and go after alien gods.

We notice that God views Israel and Judah alike. God called to himself one nation. In the course of Israel's history they had become divided, but God still has the two in mind, and so do his prophets. Any prophet who had been gripped by the traditions of Israel would have to think in this way.

2. Consider next, *the feebleness of Israel's love.* God says:

> For your loyalty is like the morning mist,
> like the dew that disappears early in the morning.

Israel's 'devotion' to God has proved to be very fleeting. The Hebrew word here is *chesed* which has already appeared in 2:19 and 4:1. Here it means loyalty, devotedness.

We know in our own lives what it means for our love to be like the early dew of morning. Our love for God is often present only in fits and starts. Many times it gives up at the slightest hint of opposition. Sometimes it tails off when people who have influenced us cease to do so. We see this, for example, in the experience of king Joash of Judah who was zealous for the things of God when the high-priest Jehoiada was around (2 Kings 12:1-2) but after Jehoiada died Joash lost his enthusiasm for these things and fell into wickedness (2 Chronicles 24:17-19). Typically, our love for God gets choked by pleasures, money and anxieties, or becomes simply a religious routine in which our fondness for God is only a matter of what we can get from him.

Love for God and love for people has to become strong and stable and firmly rooted. It gets tested. Love has to climb over obstacles. It requires determination. Love demands that we accept God and his will. It requires that we face facts and accept the other person the way he is.

This applies even to God. We must accept him the way he is. It might seem blasphemous to even think of it in any other way. Yet, often there is the wish in our hearts that God should be less demanding or more tolerant of our sins. Or, Satan paints a picture of God in our hearts in which he is pure severity. If we develop such a spirit towards God we shall find our loyalty is like the morning mist, like the early dew that disappears so swiftly.

'Devotion' to God begins by our seeing him as he is. We put aside any desire to change him. We rejoice in submitting to his holiness and purity. We set ourselves to follow and accept his will. We seek him, desiring to know what his will is.

> Cast care aside, lean on Thy guide
> Christ is Thy strength, and Christ Thy right
> ...Only believe and thou shalt see
> That Christ is all in all to Thee.[22]

---

22. The hymn 'Fight the good fight' by J.S.B. Monsell (1811-75).

It is when we 'cast care aside' and deliberately resolve to make Christ our joy, our life, our everything, that instead of our love being like rapidly evaporating dew we experience God's love like the steadily falling spring rain of Hosea 6:3.

3. Consider *the length that God has gone to*. God has given his people many privileges, but one of the greatest is that he has continued to speak to them with power.

God responds to his people's waywardness not by despairing over them, nor by violent anger, not by abandonment, but by steady determination to take action. His first action is to speak with great forcefulness.

> **⁵ Therefore I have fought them through the prophets,**
> **I have killed them with the words of my mouth.**
> **And my judgement²³ is like the light when it emerges.**

One must not imagine that this is hateful or spiteful. It is God's determination to regain his people. It is analogous to Hosea's firm treatment of his wayward wife (see 3:3).

God's way of fighting begins with his Word. It is his sword. He had sent them prophets like Elijah, and Micaiah (1 Kings 22), and Amos the contemporary of Hosea. When Israel finally fell to the Assyrians it was only after a long period of sinning against God's prophetic warnings. He 'warned them by my servants the prophets' (2 Kings 17:13). There was a living prophetic word coming to them; their sin involved despising prophetic oracles. 'They would not listen but were stubborn ...' (2 Kings 17:14-15a).

Sometimes the messages from the prophets were deadly. 'I have killed them with the words of my mouth'. God again and again made his will plain to the people of Israel, in messages and oracles that had the power of life and death in them. One thinks of the contest on Mount Carmel when fire fell from heaven at the word of

---

23. The 'k' at the end of Hebrew *wmsptyk* belongs with the next word (*k'wr*).

Elijah and false prophets were executed (1 Kings 18:36-40). The oracles of the prophets 'not only inform, but inaugurate and execute the judgement of which they tell'.[24]

God says 'And my judgement is like the light when it emerges'. God's 'judgement' is God's word, God's decision. It sheds light on our pathway. The Israelites were not able to say God had given them no guidance. His word had been like the sunrise banishing darkness, but it had not profited them.

4. Consider, *the requirement of God.* What was it that Israel lacked? What deficiency made God so unhappy with them?

⁶ For I desire mercy rather than sacrifice,
and the knowledge of God rather than burnt offerings.

Again Hosea summarises God's demand in the words 'mercy' (*chesed*) and the 'knowledge of God' (both of which we have seen already in 4:1).

Hosea's use of *chesed* has the different nuances that are found in the usage of the word generally. It includes both devotion to God and kindness to other people. In relation to God, *chesed* is piety, devotion, dedication. Hezekiah was famous for his 'acts of devotion' (2 Chronicles 32:32). Ezra asked that his 'acts of devotion' towards God should not be wiped out (Ezra 13:14).

In relation to people, *chesed* is 'loyalty' (if there is some kind of relatedness to the person) or 'mercy' (whether the person has some relationship to us or not). The Kenites showed 'mercy' to Israel when Israel was coming out of Egypt (1 Samuel 15:6), Jonathan treated David with 'kindness' (1 Samuel 20:8) and asked for 'loyal kindness' back from David (1 Samuel 20:14,15). Sometimes the emphasis is on loyalty, as the men of Jabesh-Gilead showed 'loyalty' to Saul even after he had been killed (2 Samuel 2:5) and David prayed that they would receive God's loyal kindness in return (2 Samuel 2:6). Abner also claimed to show 'loyalty' to Saul's house

---

24. J.L. Mays, *Hosea* (SCM, 1969), p.97

(2 Samuel 3:8), and David wanted to do the same (2 Samuel 9:1,3,7). David also would show loyalty to the son of someone with whom he had been in covenant (2 Samuel 10:2; 1 Chronicles 19:2). Absalom asked Hushai about his 'loyalty' to David (2 Samuel 16:17). David told Solomon to deal in loyal love to Barzillai (1 Kings 2:7).

The word also means 'mercy' or 'kindness'. Israelite kings had a reputation for 'mercy' (1 Kings 20:31). Jehoiada showed 'mercy' to Joash by saving his life when he was a child (2 Chronicles 24:22). Job spoke of those who withhold 'kindness' from a friend (Job 6:14). It is undoubtedly this aspect of the matter that meant most to the prophet Hosea and also to Micah. 'Mercy' is part of Hosea's summary of what is needed in Israel (4:1); Micah also maintained that what God required supremely was 'to do justly and to love mercy' (Micah 6:8).

It is mercy that is required rather than animal sacrifices. Hosea here is putting something above the Mosaic law. The Mosaic law required animal sacrifices. Hosea is not saying that animal sacrifices were wrong. They were required by God in Old Testament times. But he is deliberately putting something above the requirements of the law. Among the demands of the law, *chesed* ('merciful kindness') is not mentioned. Although some of the law's requirements were indeed merciful, mercy as an inward disposition is never demanded by the law. Indeed, it is against the nature of law to have much to do with mercy. In the legal sections of Exodus-Deuteronomy, mercy (*chesed*) is never mentioned except as a characteristic of God. Hosea was deliberately saying that there was something that was God's will that was *above* the Mosaic legislation, and superior to it.

It is no accident that Jesus quoted Hosea 6:6 at least twice in his short ministry (Matthew 9:13; 12:7) and alluded to it on another occasion (Matthew 23:23). The appeal, 'Have mercy', was one that seemed to have unusual power with him (Matthew 9:27; 15:22; 17:15; 20:30, 33).

Mercy is not mentioned much in the Mosaic legislation but it is part of the 'knowledge of God' which is superior to the offering of burnt offerings. True knowledge of God is not simply the accu-

mulation of data about God. 'Knowledge of God' is life-changing
awareness of his presence, practical realisation of his greatness,
empowering by his influence. One of its supreme by-products is
mercy.

Questions for Reflection

1. How much can we talk about God as if He were a human being?

2. Is there any way we can be delivered from lukewarmness in the
things of God?

3. Is mercy more important than other parts of God's will?

15. The Road To Shechem (6:7-7:2)
Hosea now comes to document some allegations he had made earlier.

> **7 But they, as at Adam[25], have broken covenant;**
> **there[26] they were treacherous against me.**

---

25. Four interpretations here invite consideration. (i) The KJV has 'they like men'.
We could paraphrase 'As is typical of people, they broke...'. (ii) Those who
believe that there was a covenant between God and Adam see a reference to it
here, and translate 'They, like Adam, transgress a covenant...'. However there is
no 'covenant' in Genesis 3, and it is without the central element in covenant-
making, the taking of an oath. (iii) Others think the translation should be 'At Adam'
or (better) 'As at Adam' and that it refers to the place called 'Adam' where Israel
crossed the Jordan (see Joshua 3:16). There is no need to emend the text for it to
mean this. Although there is no record of any special covenant at Adam which, it
is thought, was an obscure place (see D. Stuart, *Hosea-Jonah*, WBC, Word,
1987, p.99), this is not a special difficulty. Hosea is referring to a recent event. (iv)
A fourth view is that the Hebrew word for 'Adam' also means 'dirt', and the line
should be translated 'they have walked over the covenant as if it were dirt' (see
W. Kuhnigk, *Nordwestsemitische Studien zum Hoseabuch*, Biblical Institute
Press (Rome), 1974, pp. 82-85). The third view seems convincing.

26. G.A.F. Knight says 'There' might mean 'In this matter of keeping covenant'
(*Hosea: God's Love*, SCM, 1960, p. 80); this seems strained in a passage full of
place-names.

⁸ **In Gilead there is a city of evildoers,
a treacherous city, treacherous because of bloodshed.**

1. *Israelite society was murderous.* Hosea refers to a recent murderous attack, contrary to the command of the law, which took place at Adam. Apparently at the town on the river Jordan called 'Adam', about thirty kilometres from Jericho, a terrible crime took place, a breach of 'the covenant', that is the sworn agreement (see Exodus 19:8) made at Sinai. There the Israelites had sworn that they would show their loyalty to God by keeping his law, including the command against murder (Exodus 20:13). 'They' refers to the priests, as will become clear.

It was the inhabitants of Adam who were guilty of the atrocious killing, instigated, it seems, by the priests. Adam is within the district of Gilead, an area on the east side of the Jordan. The killing was presumably a political murder.

⁹ **Like those who ambush a man, like gangs,
the mob of priests commits murder on the road to Shechem.
Surely they have committed wickedness.**

When King Pekahiah was murdered, the killers had Gileadite support according to 2 Kings 15:25. This does not prove that Hosea 6:7-9 refers to the murder of Pekahiah, but it does show that Gilead had political factions in it which were capable of murder. Evidently there was some kind of political assassination at Adam and the priests were behind it.

Here are the people of God – Israel – committing major crimes. The allusions here are not just to minor misdemeanours. It is not a reference to getting angry or having impure thoughts or forgetting an act of kindness for a neighbour. The incidents mentioned in Hosea 6:7-7:2 are major transgressions of the ten commandments which were the heart and centre of the criminal law-code of Israel. Can God's people fall to such a level? Apparently they can. We recall how Paul said the name of God would become disgraced among the Gentiles because of Israel (Romans 2:24).

2. Israelite society was full of immorality.

> ¹⁰ **In the house of Israel I have seen a horrible thing.**
> **Ephraim's harlotry is there, Israel is defiled.**

How could God's people sink so low? It began by a corruption of
faith. Centuries before, around 930, Jeroboam I had put golden
statues of calves in two centres of worship, Dan and Bethel. These
were meant to represent the God who had saved Israel. Soon,
however, men and women were listening to pagan theories about
the fertility of the bulls. Then their religion allowed them to adopt
pagan sexual rites at their places of worship. But then – they thought
– if such indiscriminate sexuality was so holy there could be nothing
wrong with it in society. One's belief affects the way one lives.
People might want to abandon the God of the Bible but still live
decent lives — but it does not work that way.

Judah was as bad as Israel.

> ¹¹ **And also, Judah, for you too a harvest-time is appointed,**
> **when I turn the fortunes of my people.**

Soon the Assyrians would be swept away and only Judah would be
left. Would they learn a lesson? For them too a harvest-time – a
time when they would reap what they had sown – was appointed.
A century later Jeremiah would say, 'Have you seen what faithless
Israel did? ... She was a harlot ... Her treacherous sister Judah saw
it ... She went and became a harlot also!' (Jeremiah 3:6-8). In due
course the Judeans too would be swept away. If the Lord had not
allowed them a remnant they would have been like Sodom and
Gomorrah (Isaiah 1:9).

The phrase 'turn the fortunes' does not mean (as used to be
thought) 'turn the captivity'. It can be used with a happy meaning
or with a sad one; here the reference is negative. The prosperity of
Israel must come to an end; soon after, Judah too will have to give
account.

Soon the wickedness of Israel will be recognized.

7:1 When I heal Israel,
then the iniquity of Ephraim will be uncovered,
and so will the wickedness of Samaria.

When eventually Israel is restored then they will look back and see how ghastly their sin was. One day God will sovereignly restore Israel to faith in himself, the God of the Bible. We recall that in 1:10-2:1 God's threat of withdrawing the blessings of his relationship towards his people was followed by predictions of wonderful restoration. When such a day comes, the true nature of Israel's sin will be exposed, and they will immensely regret what they have done. Andersen is right to say: 'It is Yahweh's generosity, not his severity, that makes them ashamed of themselves'.[27]

3. *Israelite society was full of violent robbery.*

For sure, they have worked falsehood!
The thief comes,
a gang robs people in the streets.
² and they do not speak to their own hearts.
I remember all their wickedness.
Right now their deeds are all around them.
They are there before me.

In saying 'For sure, they have worked falsehood', Hosea reviews the nation's history. When Jeroboam I first put idols into his sanctuaries, his reasons were political. He seems not to have thought that he was making any great change. At that time his actions did not seem to be deep idolatry. It was just a way of picturing 'Yahweh', the God of Israel who had saved them from bondage in Egypt. It seemed to be simply an 'innocent' way of worshipping Yahweh.

But God had forbidden idols and the statues in the sanctuaries at Dan and Bethel soon became identified with all sorts of pagan religious ideas. Jeroboam's new religion continued for centuries and 'made Israel to sin' (as the books of Kings say repeatedly).

27. Andersen, *Hosea,* p. 444.

Now there is robbery in homes, gangs of muggers roam the streets. Conscience about such things has become hardened ('They do not speak to their own hearts').

And God, although amazingly patient, takes note of it all. He remembers all their wickedness, and moment-by-moment as their deeds surround them, they are also before him.

We become like the God – or the gods – that we worship. 'They went after vanity and became vanity' (Jeremiah 2:5). People may think that they can remove the worship of God and still have a decent society. Maybe they can – for a short time! But take away the God of the bible and soon the righteousness of the Bible will disappear also. Society gets steadily worse. The 'man in the street' was going on pilgrimage to Dan and to Bethel.

Two centuries after Jeroboam I came Jeroboam II. Murder and violence were everywhere, family life was broken up, immorality was the custom of the hour. 'Everyone does it. How can you be so old-fashioned?', said the people to any who protested. In their national life they had sown to the flesh, and back from the flesh they were reaping corruption.

Never was there the slightest sign of recovery for northern Israel while their idolatry continued. It kept Israel under the anger of God. God gave the northern territory over to their enemies. The nation was reduced in size and influence. Society steadily deteriorated until, now in Hosea's day, society is depraved and about to collapse altogether.

A century ago, in 'the west', men and women turned aside from the Bible. They were so confident that evolution was about to take them to the pinnacle of glory. The first world war of 1914-1918 shattered their dreams of utopia, but even that was thought to be the 'war to end all wars'. What crass ignorance of God, and ignorance of human history! The end of the twentieth century shows the re-sults: great cleverness in technology, but more murders, violence, and broken homes than ever. Lying and immorality are not even regarded as sin at all! Israel thought the nation would last for ever, but they had thirty years left. How many years does the western world have? It is one of the affluent parts of the world, but so was Israel in Jeroboam's day. Israel despised the Gentiles, but soon Assyrians and Babylonians, and then Greeks and Romans, would be far more influential and prestigious than Israel. At present 'the west' is the affluent, influential, admired part of the world. But how long will it last? The centre of gravity of the Christian world is now Africa, South America and Indonesia. One can expect Christian influence to steadily grow there as it is steadily declining in the western world.

Hosea has a message for us! The murders and the violence, the sex-craze and the lying, are signs of how much our society needs the God of the Bible. The need of the hour is not a new political party, not superior technology, not the right foreign policy, or the right relationship in some financial market. Our very survival as a people depends on whether or not spiritual awakening comes and – while we are waiting – on how many people actually come to Jesus Christ. A country with few Christians will be a place of murder, immorality and deceit. Israel proved it long ago. The modern world adds its confirmation.

Questions for Reflection

1. Can religious leaders turn to the kind of violence we find in Hosea 6:7-7:2?

2. Is it God's love or God's wrath which brings conviction of sin?

3. What are the causes of a hardened conscience?

16. The Burning Oven (7:3-7)
These verses are difficult but with some patience it is possible to tease a coherent meaning from them. Let us begin by working through the text and then we shall discern some implications for our own lives.

Hosea refers to another incident. The story picks up the last line

of Hosea 7:2. At the end of the previous short tale God said 'I
remember all their wickedness. Right now their deeds are all around
them. They are there before me'. Now there comes another incident which shows that God still has their wickedness in mind.

It is clear from reading the verses through that the picture is
one of an assassination. In Hosea's times Zechariah was murdered.
The murderer was Shallum, but he himself was killed within a month.
Menahem the killer had a reign which lasted for a few years. Pekahiah
his son was the last of his short dynasty. He was assassinated by
Pekahiah who was in turn assassinated by Hoshea (2 Kings 15:8-
31). The book of Hosea was put together after all of these events
had passed and Hosea could say 'All their kings have fallen'.

Here in Hosea 7:3-7 we are apparently looking at one of these
assassinations. It is a birthday or celebration day of some kind, the
'day of the king'. They entertain the king, then get him drunk.
They are inflamed with ambition and passion. In the early hours
of the morning the king is murdered.

To begin with, they entertain the king and his courtiers in a lewd
and deceitful way.

> **³ With their wickedness they delight the king,**
> **and with their lies they delight the princes.**

Hosea goes on to say that

> **⁴ All of them are adulterers,**
> **they are like a burning oven ²⁸.**

The line, 'All of them are adulterers', is probably to be taken
both figuratively and literally. When Hosea was told 'The land is
committing great harlotry' (1:2) the language was figurative. Yet we

---

28. Verse 4 begins, *All of them are adulterers ...,* and then the next line
in the MT has been translated: '...like an oven heated by the baker' but
there are many difficulties in this (such as a feminine adjective with a
masculine noun). Probably eight Hebrew letters should be regrouped
(the Hebrew consonants *b`rh m`ph* should be *b`r hm `ph)* and the *`ph*
('baker') should be taken to be part of the next sentence.

know that the nation's impurity was also quite a literal matter.

On this occasion they were 'burning like an oven'. This seems to refer not to sexual passion but to their burning zeal to get rid of the king and place another ruler on the throne.

There must surely be some kind of connection between the mention of the oven and the mention of the baker. This means that the next words are probably part of the simile just used.

The baker ceases to be alert,
he leaves off from kneading the dough,
leaving it until it is leavened.

The baker has been kneading the dough, pummelling, rolling, stretching and squeezing it, and so spreading the yeast evenly throughout the dough. Then he covers it and leaves it to rise. When it has risen he puts it into a hot oven. The dough has to be leavened before it is put into a large oven to be baked.

In Hosea's illustration, however, the baker ceases to be alert (as the Hebrew may be translated[29]) and having left off kneading the dough, he falls asleep. Meanwhile the oven has become dangerously ablaze.

I take this to be a development of the words, 'like a burning oven'. It is as if Hosea says: 'Imagine a baker ceasing to pay attention to what he is doing. He forgets to control the oven. He kneads the dough, and then stops doing so and leaves it to rise. He then falls asleep leaving the fire of the oven unattended. By morning time it is a blazing inferno'.

The wild party – or whatever it was – was much the same. The would-be assassins entertained the king. As the night wore on, the king became more helpless but the assassins became more wildly ambitious. By the early hours of the morning they were in a burning rage against the king.

---

29. Andersen, *Hosea*, p.457.

⁵**On the day of our king,**
the princes made him sick with the warmth of wine.
He was welcoming friendship with scornful people.

The Hebrew here is literally 'He pulled his hands with scorners';
it seems to be an idiom for welcoming friendship. In his drunken
foolishness the king was welcoming the friendship of those who
were about to kill him. At this stage of the night the king's enemies
were ablaze with consuming passion and were about to throw caution aside. Their flaming rage was ready for murder.

⁶**When they drew near their hearts were like an oven, as they were**
plotting.

Again Hosea develops the illustration:

All the night their baker was sleeping.
In the morning the oven is burning like a flaming fire.
⁷ **All of them became heated like an oven,**
and they devoured their judges.

The language is still applying Hosea's 'burning oven' illustration.
In the early morning their ambition and hatred were fanned into
flame. The assassins were ablaze with hate and determination. They
killed their drunken king and his colleagues.
    Hosea adds a comment.

All their kings have fallen.
There is no one among them that calls upon me.

We can draw some conclusions for ourselves from the sketch we
have here of the condition of Israel at that time.

1. *Here is a picture of the direction in which godless leadership is*
likely to move. Israel had moved away from the favour of God
when two centuries earlier it had deliberately adopted idolatry as its
national way of life. Now we are seeing the end-product of that
decision. Pagan leadership becomes nothing but a mixture of pas-

sion, drunkenness and ambition. Generally speaking, only faith in the God of the bible prevents national leaders from steadily declining into a riot of profligacy and ambition. Rulers without God misuse their position, wealth, opportunities and power, and ruin their country.

2. *We have in our brief story an insight into human nature.* Behind this account of intrigue and assassination is a description of the nature of the human heart. It gets aroused, and inflamed, and can be brought to do incredibly wicked things. It loses its ability to think straight.

In our vignette, the king's enemies are already wicked and willing to deceive in order to fulfil their ambitions ('With their wickedness they delight the king ...'). They are already deep in idolatry and all that it brings ('All of them are adulterers...'). But over and above that, the circumstances of the day have roused their ambitions and their emotions. They are now like an oven becoming increasingly out of control. It has been left to blaze and is now an inferno.

Men and women like to think of themselves as intelligent and as sensible people in control of their lives and making sensible decisions. But the truth is wholly otherwise: we are governed not by calm and cool intelligence but by our feelings, resentments and ambitions. 'They are like a burning oven', says Hosea, and it is a description of the way any member of the human race can go when the circumstances lead that way.

We are not as rational as we think! Put under sufficient pressure, any one of us can become 'burning like a flaming fire'. A turn-about comes when we give our bodies to God and are transformed by the renewing of our minds. Then clarity comes and the 'blazing oven' can be cooled down. We get to know the good and acceptable and perfect will of God (see Romans 12:12). We can control the 'blazing oven' of our own nature and are given 'the Spirit of a sound mind' (2 Timothy 1:7).

3. *Hosea points to the inevitable failure of society without God.*
The scene Hosea sketches, points us to the need of a Saviour. In
the gospel of Jesus Christ there is provision for being 'transformed
by the renewing of your minds'. Without Christ, paganism at its
best flows downhill and destroys itself as Israel was about to destroy
itself with its repeated assassinations. The nation devoured its own
judges, and all their kings fell. A different scenario can come only
by the power of the risen Lord Jesus Christ.

Many societies of the world bear great resemblance to Hosea's
little picture. The idea in some circles seems to be that international
leadership can proceed by calm, cool, rational decisions, and that
the spreading of democracy throughout the world will soon bring
peace and prosperity everywhere. What nonsense! The world's
philosophers and statesmen forget the spiritual side of leadership,
and forget that in the inter-play of ambitions and rivalries, leaders
become 'burning like a flaming fire'.

There can be no stable society unless idolatry is removed. No
doubt if the various political factions of Israel had been interviewed
they would have given their reasons for being in favour of the king,
or reasons for seeking his removal. They would have perhaps chat-
ted glibly about the state of the nation, and so on. But the truth was
that Israel had been on a downhill course ever since the day when
Jeroboam had placed idols in his two sanctuaries. Since the day
when Jeroboam had set his face against Jerusalem, Israel had deteriorated. Since the day when Jeroboam I had been determined to
stop any of his people going to worship Yahweh, the God who had
given promises to the house of David, since that day, Israel had
steadily declined. Step number one in any recovery would have
been the renunciation of idolatry. While the nation continued its
idolatries its doom was sealed. They really committed national
suicide. 'All their kings have fallen' – at the hands of their own
citizens.

4. *The deepest reason for failure is prayerlessness and unbelief.* Hosea's final comment at the end of this short unit is: 'No one among them calls upon me'. One would think that with such a crisis on its hands the nation would have turned to its God, but they were far removed from doing that. Two centuries of departure from the God of Abraham, Isaac and Jacob had brought them to a state where it did not even occur to them to call upon Yahweh, the God who long before had delivered them by the blood of a lamb.

Prayerlessness was the cause. Later on, Hosea will point to prayerfulness as the answer: 'Take words with you and return to Yahweh' (14:2).

Questions for Reflection

1. Is human nature like an out-of-control fire?

2. Is it true that the cause of all spiritual problems is prayerlessness?

3. Can God give his people something he disapproves of?

17. Mixed-Up and Half-Baked (7:8-16)

[8] **Ephraim! He mixes himself with the nations.**
Ephraim has become a cake cooked only on one side.
[9] **Foreigners have devoured his strength**
and he has not realised it.
Fungus is here and there upon him,
but he has not realised it.
[10] **Israel's pride will testify against it.**
They have not turned to Yahweh their God,
nor have they sought him in all of this.
[11] **So Ephraim has become like a silly senseless dove.**
They call to Egypt, they go to Assyria.
[12] **As they go away, I will throw my net over them;**
I will bring them down like the birds of the sky.

At the sound of their clustering together I will capture them.[30]
[13]Woe to them, for they have strayed from me!
Destruction is coming to them,
for they have rebelled against me!
I redeemed them, but they on their part speak lies against me.
[14] And they do not cry to me from their heart
when they howl on their beds.
For the sake of grain and new wine they slash themselves;[31]
but they are turning away from me.
[15] I was the one who trained them,
I was the one who strengthened their arms,
yet they consider me to be evil.[32]
[16]They turn around, but not to the Most High,[33]
They are like a treacherous bow.

---

30. The Hebrew *'ysrm* is difficult; Andersen thinks the line is 'almost unintelligible' (*Hosea*, p. 469). A comparison of Hosea 7:12 and 10:10 suggests that *ysr* and *'sr* were confused or were interchangeable in the northern Israelite dialect of Hosea. The spelling seems the wrong way round compared to what we would expect in these two verses. It seems that *ysr* here has the sense of *'sr* which is used of holding prisoner (Genesis 39:20; 40:3, 5; 42:24) and of tying an animal (2 Kings 7:10). It makes perfect sense when used of capturing birds. If *sm'* is read as *sema'* and means 'sound' (as in Psalm 150:5), and *'edah* means 'swarming together' (as in Judges 14:8, where it is used of bees), then it should be translated as above, without emendation of the consonantal text. A similar but not identical interpretation is found in C. Van Gelderen and W. H. Gispen, *Het Boek Hosea* (Kok, 1953), pp. 261-262.

31. The ancient Greek translation provides evidence that the verb *gdd* was misread as the verb *grr*. The letters *r* and *d* are close in Hebrew script; this reading is widely accepted.

32. The Hebrew *chashab 'el* means 'to attribute something to someone', rather than 'to devise something against someone'. To devise something *against* someone is *chashab 'al*. The Hebrew here is *chashab 'el*; it is close to *chashab l* in 1 Samuel 1:13 ('Eli reckoned her to be a drunken woman').

33. The Hebrew here has some kind of name. I take it that *'Al* is related to *'Elyon*, 'God Most High'.

> **Their princes will fall by the sword,**
> **because of God's anger at what they say.**[34]
> **In the land of Egypt, the people will talk about them with**
> **derision.**

Hosea turns to scornful and derisive descriptions of the sin of Israel.

1. *Sin confuses.* Israel is mixed up – in more than one sense. 'He mixes himself with the nations', says Hosea. Israel blends in with the nations so as to be just like them. As far back as the days of Samuel, they wanted to be 'like all the nations' (1 Samuel 8:5). Idolatry always strips the people of God of their distinctiveness. They become intermingled with paganism so as to lose their distinctiveness. Then they are mixed-up within themselves as they try to feel at home with worldly ways and yet they have a past in which God has spoken to them.

2. *Sin in God's people obstructs his work in their lives.* 'Ephraim has become a cake cooked only on one side'. Presumably baking in the ancient world involved turning the cake round at some stage of the cooking. Otherwise the cake would be burnt on one side and raw on the other.

God has not been allowed to finish his work with Israel. He is like a baker who starts cooking but leaves the cake unattended in the middle of the work. The result is that the cake is spoiled, shrivelled on one side, uncooked on the other and altogether useless. Sin in God's people means that God's plan is unfulfilled at present, and that they are rendered useless to him.

3. *Sin brings deprivation and weakness.* 'Foreigners have devoured his strength, and he has not realised it'. Like a man who is past his prime, Israel's best days have gone. By turning to idolatry Israel had lost her greatness. Idolatry has brought nothing but impoverish-

---

34. This is literally 'the rage at their tongue'. The Hebrew for 'rage' is always used of God's anger.

ment. Crime grips the country. The extent of the territory has shrunk.

Not that Israel realised any of this. They had dreams of security in the advantages that came to them because they were allied to a great nation like Assyria.

Today's believers who turn to today's little pagan gods, similarly lose their zeal and their distinctiveness, and become like Samson who lost his strength without realising it, and found that previous victories were now only a memory.

4. *Sin brings decay*.

Fungus is here and there upon him,
but he has not realised it.

The Hebrew word here means 'fungus' not grey hair as in older translations. Grey hair was respected!

The picture is of bread that has gone mouldy, implying smelly deterioration in the state of the nation. Israel had once been a prestigious and prosperous nation. Its prestige was the result of the blessing of God. When Solomon gave himself to God with a thousand burnt offerings (1 Kings 3:4), he did not know that because of his seeking first God's kingdom innumerable blessings would ensue, making his empire the greatest of his day. Within his own lifetime the 'glory of Solomon' was famous. But now the nation is mouldy and does not realise it.

5. *Sin brings pride*. Without using any imagery, Hosea gives warning.

¹⁰ **Israel's pride will testify against it.**
They have not turned to Yahweh their God,
nor have they sought him in all of this.

The nation's pride was seen in its prayerless self-sufficiency. One might not think that prayerlessness was a fault of Israel. They went to many religious meetings! They also wailed to God on their beds (7:14). But Hosea does not regard this as true prayer. They were not truly consulting God's will, nor truly asking that his kingdom might come in the life of their nation. No doubt there was wailing because of the troubles they were in, and there were requests for fertility in their land, but they were not truly seeking Yahweh.

6. *Sin is silliness*. Hosea uses the picture of a dove frantically hopping here and there. Israel is like a bird pecking here, pecking there, unaware of the hunting net. At one time it is an ally to Egypt, at another time an ally to Assyria – and yet Assyria and Egypt were enemies. Israel was deceived, for security was not to be found in either!

So God would treat them like a dove. The next time they flew into the air in the direction of Assyria or Egypt, God would throw his bird-hunting net over them!

The answer to the needs of mankind now, as then, does not lie with the next superpower that comes along, but in submission to the God of Abraham, Isaac and Jacob. Sin is ridiculous, silly, culpably insane.

7. *Sin is ingratitude*. The emphasis in 7:13 is upon the sheer goodness of God to the nation. 'They have strayed from me ... they have rebelled against me! On God's side there was redemption. The Hebrew is emphatic: What *I* did was redeem them; *they* for their part speak lies against me.

Sin in God's people is always ingratitude. In the periods of history where godly influences are high, it does so much good. Israel had been redeemed by the blood of the lamb. God had provided for them everything necessary for their growth. He had sent his word to them again and again. He had restored them many times. On his side there was redemption, but it did not meet with the corresponding faith on their side.

8. *Sin is selfishness and insincerity.*

> They do not cry to me sincerely,
> when they howl on their beds ...

There was plenty of praying in Israel. Sometimes when the people
were in trouble they would howl and weep and call out to Yahweh
who had saved them in days gone by. Sincere distress, God will
heed. But Israel's screaming prayers were not contrition, they were
not hunger for God. No one is an atheist when he is in trouble.
They were not interested in coming under the direction of God;
they simply wanted an easier life and better harvests. Like the pagan praying of 1 Kings 18:28, they would slash themselves to im-
press God, but it did no good. An unbroken and an impenitent heart
God will despise.

9. *Sin misrepresents God*. It prevents us from seeing God as he
really is. On the one hand we act as if God will take no notice of us.
On the other hand we fear him and regard him as malevolent towards us. The truth is that God is as Hosea saw him through his
painful experience of a traumatic marriage. God says

> [15] **I was the one who trained them**
> **and strengthened their arms,**
> **yet they have reckoned me to be evil.**

They had found no evil in God. He had always dealt with them in
tenderness. In the early days of the nation he had gradually trained
them to stand for God amidst other nations. Their present fears
were the side-effect of their guilt-feelings.

10. *Sin is turning to what is worthless*. There was much changing
of position within Israel. They were like a silly dove, hopping this
way, hopping that way. But they never moved in the direction of
God. 'They turn around, but not to the Most High'. They were
unreliable, as when a warrior in the battle field turns to use his
bow but finds it slack and useless.

Soon the end of the nation will come. 'Their princes will fall
by the sword'. God is giving last calls and last warnings. He is
angry at their disbelief, their idolatry, their misrepresentation of

his character. He is angry at what they say. Soon the whole world will know of their defect. 'In the land of Egypt – the very place from which they had been redeemed – the people will talk about them with derision'. God's punishment will involve disgrace – unless they back out of their folly in these remaining moments of their history.

Questions for Reflection

1. Can there be useless praying?

2. How does sin bring confusion?

3. What are today's 'little pagan gods'?

18. Calves and Kings (8:1-8)

Hosea 8:1 to 11:11 focuses on events in Israel's spiritual history. The first matter, in 8:1-8, is the rebelliousness of Israel in choosing kings and in choosing gods for themselves.

Hosea begins with (1) *a call to face the situation and realise God's wrath is at hand.*

> **¹ Put the trumpet to your mouth!**
> **Like a vulture someone is over the house of Yahweh!**

Hosea calls upon a watchman to blast the trumpet to warn that an invading enemy is coming. It is a symbolic way of announcing the judgement of God. The house of Israel – the entire northern nation – is like a dying man and a vulture is circling round waiting to swoop. The language is poetical; the encircling vulture is no doubt the Assyrian threat. Deportation is at hand.

> **The reason is that they have transgressed my covenant,**
> **and have rebelled against my law.**

Covenant is often thought to be simply some kind of bond or commitment or agreement, but it is important to define covenant in a way that takes note of its central ingredient: the taking of an oath. 'Covenant' is a promise or promises which have become legally binding by the taking of an oath. There are different types of covenant but they fall into three groups according to who takes the oath. In a promissory covenant a senior partner or benefactor swears some blessing or benefaction for a junior. In a parity covenant two equals exchange oaths. In a covenant of loyalty, a senior partner imposes his requirements upon a junior. The Mosaic covenant was a covenant of law; all other covenants where God is a partner are covenants of generosity and he takes the oath. When the covenant of Sinai is in mind 'covenant' and 'law' are virtually synonyms. In other types of covenant this is not so, and detailed law is not to be found.

God's relationship to Israel was *initiated* by redemption through blood. It was *maintained* by obedience to Mosaic law. The nation was promised life if it kept the Mosaic law. The 'life' concerned was not 'eternal life' as we have it in the New Testament but 'living long in the land' as we have it in the fifth commandment.

The equivalent of the Mosaic law for the Christian is walking in the Spirit. Jesus's death came at the time of the Passover and was the fulfilling of Passover. The Spirit was given at Pentecost, fifty days after the Passover and at the time when the giving of the law was celebrated. Instead of giving a new law, God gave the Spirit. When we have faith in a crucified and risen Saviour we are not under the Mosaic Passover; we 'fulfil' it. Likewise when we walk in the Spirit we are not under the Mosaic legislation; rather we 'fulfil' it. The morality of the law is not lost. It is kept and more-than-kept by walking in the Holy Spirit.

With this adaptation Hosea's principles are all relevant for the modern Christian. The Christian must be careful not to break God's new covenant of generosity which involves walking in the Spirit. Under the old covenant the Israelite kept the law and 'lived long in the land'. If he did not do so, he faced exile and loss of territory.

Under the covenant of the blood of Jesus, the believer must walk in the Spirit. By doing so, from the Holy Spirit he 'reaps' eternal life, that is, he enjoys the actual experience of eternal life. If in the lives of Christians it can be said that 'they have transgressed my covenant, and have rebelled against my law' (of walking in the Spirit), the Christian, like the Israelite, will find that the Lord will judge his people and that it is a fearful thing to fall into the hands of the living God (Hebrews 10:30, 31). 'Anyone who set aside the Law' was punished; 'severe punishment' comes when the Christian has 'insulted the Spirit' (Hebrews 10:28-29).

Next comes (2) *an accusation of hypocrisy*.

² **They cry out to me,**
'God of[35] **Israel, we know you!'**
³ **Israel has rejected the good;**
an enemy pursues him.

Israel had a flourishing religious life. Plenty of praying went on in wicked, northern Israel. They even rejoiced in their supposed knowledge of God. But the religion was just that – ritualistic self-centred religiosity. It was not love of God. Israel had 'rejected the good'. Often 'the good' in a covenant context has the idea of the blessings of the covenant, the results that would flow from their obedience to the law. Despite Israel's claimed relationship to God, they were not keeping the Mosaic law and were thus forfeiting the 'life and the good' that came from obedience (Deuteronomy 30:15). The result of their disobedience was that an enemy was encircling the land like a vulture – the Assyrians.

Next comes (3) the specific charges, notably *self-will in choosing leadership and in choosing one's own god*.

---

35. The vowel-pointing of the Hebrew should be emended to yield 'God-of' (the construct state). It is a 'broken construct chain'.

> [4]They have set up kings, but not through me.
> They have appointed princes, but I did not acknowledge them.
> With their silver and their gold they made for themselves idols.
> As a result Israel[36] will be cut off.
> [5]He has rejected your calf, O Samaria.
> No anger burns against them!
> How long will they be incapable of purity?
> [6] For this thing comes from Israel!
> A craftsman made it, so it is not God.
> Surely the calf of Samaria will be broken in pieces.

We have seen already the story of northern Israel's way of choosing leadership. In its history from 931 to 723 there were nineteen kings, seven of whom were assassinated, and one of whom committed suicide. After Jeroboam's death in 753, there were two assassinations in the year 752 and two more in 742-740. In the time Hosea was preaching, assassination had become a way of life! Israel had a tradition of being given its leaders by God. Saul was a God-given leader (however badly he may have used his opportunity). So was David and the entire line of Judean kings, the 'sons of David'. In the north, God had predicted and approved the kingship of Jeroboam I and had offered him a stable line (1 Kings 11:38). Jehu – for all his violence – was God-appointed (1 Kings 19:16). But now Israel had thrown all of that aside. There was no question now of looking for the right leaders from God. Ungodly men simply rose up, assassinated the king and took over. Finding the leader became a matter of human expediency, ingenuity and violence.

Something similar took place with divine leadership also. 'With their silver and their gold they *made for themselves* idols'. Just as a God-appointed leader was of no interest to them, so God's appointment of himself as their leader was also of no interest to them.

Hosea spells out the consequences. (i) It would lead to the end of the nation ('Israel will be cut off'). (ii) The 'new theology' would

---

36. In the Hebrew the subject is 'it'. The singular most likely refers to Israel.

be rejected ('He has rejected your calf, O Samaria'). (iii) They would face God's anger ('My anger burns ...'), because their idolatry was evidence of long-term rejection of God himself, and of persistent wickedness. How long would they be incapable of purity? It was a scandal that such an idol as the golden calf they were using should be made in Israel. Had they learned nothing from the story of Aaron's 'golden calf' at Sinai? But 'this thing comes from Israel!'. It was man-made, not truly divine, doomed to judgement. 'Surely the calf of Samaria will be broken in pieces'.

Fourthly we have *the threat of judgement* but in terms of a reaping-and-sowing metaphor.

> [7] **For they sow when it is windy,**
> **and they will reap in a storm.**
> **Grain will not have new growth;**
> **it will not make a meal.**
> **If it does, foreigners will consume it.**

The phrase here is not 'sowing the wind' (an unintelligible idea) and 'reaping the whirlwind'. Rather it is a way of speaking of total uselessness, speaking in agricultural imagery. They are sowing grain in impossible conditions. 'They sow when it is windy'. What good can be achieved living the way they are living? They will reap in a situation where nothing can be reaped! They will reap in a storm.

The agricultural metaphor goes on. It is humorously illogical! They are sowing when they cannot sow. They are reaping in situations where they cannot reap. If there is any grain it will not produce any shoots of growth. If there is any seed reaped it will not make a meal. And if it does make a meal it will be snatched away as it is about to be eaten and a foreigner will eat it!

There could not be a greater way of ridiculing Israel's position and showing its total worthlessness. The gain that they are achieving is nil. Their gods are totally useless to save them in trouble, to help them in need, or to avert the anger of God which will fall upon them any moment now.

> ⁸ **Israel is swallowed up.**
> **They are now among the nations,**
> **like a jar in which no one delights.**

Centuries before, Israel had wanted a king to be 'like the nations'. The kingship of God was not good enough for them. Now they have got what they wanted, and are totally 'swallowed up', 'among the nations'. It was what they wanted kingship for in the first place!

It is often that way. Like Lot in Genesis 19:20, we want something intensely. This is near! This is at hand! Never mind about unseen ambitions for God. Let me have this. I want to be like everyone else. 'Is it not a little one?' God says 'Alright, I grant you this request' (see Genesis 19:21) but when we have our request it is not worth having! So Israel said 'Please let us have a king. Please let us be like the nations' (1 Samuel 8). They got their king and the northern half of the nation went on getting its kings and its gods as it wanted. But the end-result was clear. They were 'a jar in which no one delights', a once beautiful nation now ruined and on the verge of extinction.

Would anyone take notice of Hosea? 'If any one person hears my voice', said Jesus, 'I will come in to him' (see Revelation 3:20).

Questions for Reflection

1. Was Hosea a successful prophet?

2. Should the Christian think much about his country's history?

3. Do political crises come from God?

19. Bad Company, Bad Habits (8:9-14)

The next aspect of Israel's spiritual history to receive Hosea's comment is the nation's making of alliances with paganism. Assyria's gods are bad company for Israel to keep, and will lead to disaster in the nation's life.

1. *It is a mistake to seek security in friendship with idolatry.* Israel tied itself up with the paganism of Assyria.

> ⁹ **Indeed they have gone up to Assyria.**
> **Ephraim is a wild donkey all alone.**
> **They have hired lovers.**
> ¹⁰ **And surely they hire lovers among the nations.**

The rulers of northern Israel at one point turned to Assyria to make a political alliance with it. We are reminded of Menahem's dependence on Assyria (2 Kings 15:19-20).

Hosea regards this as spiritual idolatry. It is turning to the gods of Assyria and being unfaithful to Yahweh. Wild donkeys were proverbial for lustfulness (see Jeremiah 2:24). In its craving for gods other than the LORD, Israel is 'a wild donkey all alone' and wanting a lover. 'Ephraim has *hired* lovers', says Hosea, most probably referring to the fact that Menahem had to make payment of money to get Assyria's support.

> **Now I will gather them up;**
> **and they will soon writhe in pain³⁷**
> **because of the burden of the king of princes.**

God will gather Israel for judgement (see the word 'gather' in Joel 3:11 and elsewhere). They will soon be in extreme distress because of 'the burden' – the demands, financial and otherwise – of 'the king of princes', the Assyrian king.

Our friends and allies always have an impact upon us for good or bad. Every society needs to keep a balance between friendship

---

37. The line 'and they will soon writhe in pain' is difficult to translate. Is the verb related to 'becoming ill' (as in 7:5)? Or does it mean 'to writhe in agony'? Does it mean 'to begin'? Does 'a little' mean 'a little time' or 'to a little extent'? The 'king of princes' seems to be the equivalent of the Assyrian title 'king of kings'. The 'burden' must be the imposed payment Israel must make. So the translation that fits best is the one suggested.

and watchfulness. Friendships within the community of the nations are desirable. Every effort needs to be made to foster mutual understanding among the nations. Of course! Why build enmity needlessly? Yet at the same time a country with a large number of Christians in it, and similarly the individual Christian, needs to watch that their relationship to God stays firm.

2. *Carelessness about God can be combined with religious zeal.*
Israel's alliance with Assyria drew the nation into Assyria's religious customs. Evidently at this time there was a flood of altar-building.

**¹¹ Surely Ephraim has multiplied altars for removing sin[38],
but they have become for him altars of sinning.**

Israel's sacrificial system was designed to give a partial and symbolic eradication of the stain caused by sin. It was only partial; it did not cover major crimes. And it was only symbolic, 'a shadow ... not the very reality of the things themselves' (Hebrews 10:1). Assyrian sacrificial practice was probably somewhat different but the overall intent was the same: to forestall the god's anger and to retain his goodwill.

But their building of altars was bound up with Assyrian idolatry. So many altars, so many sins! Like Ahaz who built altars, but only for Canaanite deities, so now Israel is building many altars – but only for the support of Assyrian religion. False alliances are corrupting. Israel may have wanted to be allied to Assyria for reasons of political security, but 'bad company corrupts good morals', and the alliance served more to foment Israel's love of strange gods.

3. *Carelessness about God combined with religious zeal generally shows contempt for God's written word.* Hosea writes:

---

38. It has been long recognized that the Hebrew verb here can mean 'to sin' or 'to remove sin'. See for example, W. Rudolph, *Hosea* (Kommentar zum Alten Testament, Gerd Mohn, 1966), p. 167.

> [12] **I wrote for him many requirements[39] in my law;**
> **they are regarded as a strange thing.**

For Hosea the Israelites spent time and energy on religious ritual but disregarded God's written word. 'Religiosity' gets its own ideas for its religious traditions, and follows any teacher who is persuasive, but it neglects the written word of God. It seems easier to follow current ideas or what the latest prophet might happen to be saying. To attend to a written document takes more trouble. It was fashionable in Hosea's time to follow the religious customs of the Assyrians.

Ordinary people attend more to what they hear than to what they read. The priests of Israel – like the preachers of today – were to draw attention to the written Word of God, and were to expound orally what was in the law of Moses in written form.

Hosea has already charged the priests with failing to teach God's written law (4:6), and has said that the people break the written requirements of God's covenant with Israel (8:1). Special attention is drawn to the quantity of requirements. Exodus-Deuteronomy has about two thousand verses of legislation. They were compacted into ten – the 'Ten Commandments'. Jesus could summarise them in two (Matthew 22:37-39). When the Spirit was outpoured on the church and 'life in the Spirit' was raised to a higher level, the central focus becomes *one* requirement: 'it is summed up in this word: you shall love your neighbour...' (Romans 13:9). In the movement from 'law' to 'Spirit', there is a change of emphasis. The focus is no longer on Moses' legislation; the focus is on Jesus, the Holy Spirit, the requirement of love. However, the change is not to be exaggerated. If it is important not to substitute the Bible in the place of the Holy Spirit, it is also important not to think the Holy Spirit renders the Bible unnecessary. The written Word of God – although it is to be read 'in the Spirit' is still to be read and attended to, lest Hosea be re-written 'I wrote for him many requirements in

---

39. The noun *rbw* or *rby* is unknown but its connection with the root *rb* gives it an obvious meaning, 'multitude'.

the life of the Holy Spirit, but they are regarded as a strange thing'.
Israel gave itself to Assyrian-influenced religion, but it did them no
good and did not secure the blessing of God.

> [13] **They offer the sacrifices of my burnt-offerings,**[40]
> **they sacrifice flesh and they eat;**
> **but Yahweh has taken no delight in them.**
> **Now he will punish their iniquity,**
> **and punish them for their sins;**
> **they will return to Egypt.**

The Israelites often participated in the system of offering regular
animal-sacrifices. Religious meals involving animal-sacrifices had
been part of their way of life for centuries. But the system was
now contaminated with Assyrian idolatry, and they were careless
about the Mosaic law. The result of religion that did not relate to
God's written Word was loss of God's approval ('Yahweh has taken
no delight in them'), punishment for God-less religion ('he will punish them'), and the loss of their experience of deliverance from
Egypt ('they will return to Egypt').

The last line of verse 13 is shattering in its intensity. Despite all
the wickedness of Israel over many years, the undoing of their
redemption was not generally threatened. When the first generation
of Israelites experienced the oath of God's wrath, and God refused
to allow them to enter Canaan, they were not taken back to Egypt.

---

40. There is a word *habhab* in late Hebrew that has to do with roasting. If
the verb 'sacrifice' does double-duty; if 'sacrifices of my *habhabim*' is
the object of the double-duty verb; and if *hbhb* refers to a sacrificed
animal (as is likely if it is the object of 'sacrifice'), then the sense will be:
They offer sacrifices of my burnt-offerings. Calvin took the words to mean
'sacrificia holocaustorum meorum' ('sacrifices of my burnt offerings')
over four centuries ago, following earlier interpreters who reckoned that
habhabim meant 'sacrifices either burnt or roasted'. See J. Calvin, *Commentaries on the Twelve Minor Prophets,* vol. 1 (Banner of Truth reprint,
1986), p. 302. Rudolph (in *Hosea*, p. 160) and Van Gelderen (in *Hosea*,
pp. 304-307) mention a range of possibilities.

They lost that for which they were redeemed, for a generation, but they were not 'un-redeemed'. The blood of the lamb which saved them in Egypt was not put into reverse. They lost Canaan for a generation, but they did not go back to Egyptian bondage. Rather they stayed in the wilderness.

Hosea speaks of something worse than staying in the wilderness: 'they will return to Egypt'. Hosea is using figurative language; Israel was never literally exiled to Egypt. He is referring to something temporary, for we have seen rich promises in Hosea 2:14-23. And he refers to *national* loss-of-redemption rather than lost salvation for any individual. For a community may lose its position as part of God's church without there being loss of salvation for any individual. The children may not have the faith that their parents had. This is the point of Romans 11:17-20 and Revelation 2:5.

For the moment it will be as if they were un-redeemed. Northern Israel will for centuries be no part of the people of God, and be excluded from all that will take place in Judah. Not until Jesus comes will the people who sit in darkness (in northern Israel) see a great light.

4. *Religion without submission to God or fellowship with him may have its projects and programmes, but they will be destined for extermination.* Israel was building its temples but God was neglected.

> **¹⁴ For Israel has forgotten its maker and built temples;**
> **and Judah has multiplied fortified cities.**
> **But I will send a fire on its cities**
> **that it may consume its palatial dwellings.**

The Hebrew word for 'temple' may also mean 'palace' so the reference here could be to building luxurious residences, but since Israel was 'multiplying altars' (8:11) it is likely that the reference is to religious buildings as well.

It took time and effort to construct these buildings, but the nation was taking no time and putting forth no effort to seek God!

This shows what absorbed Israel's energies. The nation's religion was not interested in God as he really is; it was simply a matter of superstition and self-protection.

Israel was wandering far from God. Its false alliances, its insincerity and disregard for God's written Word, its preoccupation with projects and programmes but neglect of God, would all be disastrous and the whole lot would soon be swept away.

What is needed in our lives is not false coalitions but distinctiveness, not carelessness but attentiveness to God's written Word, preoccupation with God and his righteousness and his will. 'They were broken off for their unbelief; you stand only by faith' (Romans 11:20).

Questions for Reflection

1. Should our country avoid alliances with other countries?

2. Does expounding God's Word really produce spirituality?

3. Can the church be unredeemed?

20. Lost Inheritance (9:1-9)
When we turn from God to empty and man-made religiosity, however traditional it may be, (i) we lose our inheritance, (ii) we lose true worship, and (iii) we lose the experience of having our inward eyes enlightened (Ephesians 1:18). These are the themes of this section of Hosea.

1. *Without him, God's people lose their inheritance.*
Hosea says:

> ¹ **Do not rejoice, O Israel,**
> **do not be jubilant like the nations!**
> **For you have played the harlot, forsaking your God.**
> **For on every threshing floor you have made love**
> **to get harlots' pay.**

'Rejoice' represents a Hebrew word that is often used of dancing or joy in worship. Here it refers to pagan worship.

All of the nations around Israel had their religions. Israel was not meant to be like them, but to be distinct from them. Israel's faith was not simply to be a matter of following religious customs like everyone else. The nation had received a revelation from Yahweh. God had saved them by the blood of a lamb, and by saving them revealed his name and his nature to them. But now they are in spiritual adultery. Like a harlot having sex with men on every convenient heap of grain, so the populace of Israel adopts the religious fashions coming from prestigious Assyria. The intent was to prosper the crops and benefit the animals, but the result will be that the land of Israel will fail them.

> [2] **Threshing floor and wine press will not feed them,**
> **and the new wine will fail them.**

Israel turned to Canaanite and Assyrian religious ideas because these seemed to hold out better hope of prosperity. After all, Assyria was doing rather well politically, and it was the richest country around. It seemed a good idea to copy the nation whose religion held out hope of earthly riches.

Human wickedness always wants to make a prosperity cult out of the worship of God. Faith gets twisted so that its main aim is not to bring forgiveness, righteousness and the service of God, but to get help to pay the rent, prosper the farm, get rapid promotion and improve the business! 'Seek first the kingdom of God and his righteousness, and all these things shall be added ...' becomes 'Seek ye first all the financial help God can give and we shall be enthusiastic about his kingdom and be more zealous in the meetings – provided his help keeps coming'.

It does not work. 'Threshing floor and wine press' – the business endeavours Israel was concerned about – 'will not feed them, and the new wine will fail them'.

Worse still, if the nation did not speedily repent, Israel would lose her inheritance altogether.

> ³ **They will not remain in Yahweh's land,**
> **but Ephraim will return to Egypt,**
> **and in Assyria they will eat unclean food.**

The land of Israel was Israel's inheritance. 'Listen to the statutes of the law', said God through Moses, 'in order that you may ... take possession of the land' (Deuteronomy 4:1). 'Do what is right and good ... that you may ... inherit the good land' (Deuteronomy 6:18).

Disobedience would bring disinheritance. 'If you are not careful to obey all the words of this law ... Yahweh will scatter you among the peoples ... Yahweh will bring you back to Egypt in ships' (Deuteronomy 28:58, 64, 68). Seeking God for the purpose of prosperity fails – and results in a perverted pagan view of God.

For the Christian the principle stays the same: 'Those who practise such things shall not *inherit* ...'. Only, what is inherited is not land but rather a realm of peace, usefulness, experience of the kingdom, consciousness of God's favour.

In Israel's case the people would be removed from Israel. They would figuratively speaking 'go back to Egypt' from which they had been redeemed. The reality was that they would find themselves deported to Assyria. There are equivalents to this for the Christian. When the believer turns from God, he loses his 'inheritance', the life of usefulness and of peace and of the presence of God. It is *as though* he were unredeemed – although God's purpose is not broken – and he is as if in Assyria eating unclean food. His inheritance is lost albeit temporarily.

2. *Without him, God's people lose true worship.* When judgement falls upon Israel as the Assyrians invade the land, the people will lose the privilege of worshipping Yahweh altogether.

> ⁴ **They will not pour out offerings of wine to Yahweh,**
> **nor will they offer their sacrifices to him.**
> **Surely[41] the bread of mourners will be theirs;**

41. There is an asseverative *kaph* here (see R. Gordis, The Asseverative Kaph in Ugaritic and Hebrew, *JAOS*, 63, 1943, pp.176-178). It is not necessary to read *ki*.

all who eat it will be defiled.
Truly their bread will be to keep themselves alive;
no one will enter the domain of Yahweh.

When the people of Israel face deportation, they will not be able to pour out offerings of wine to Yahweh, as a sign of self-surrender. They will be cut off from the sacrificial system altogether when they are deported to strange lands.

In the place to which they are deported, they will be like those who are at a funeral. Their food will be like that which is provided at a meeting for the bereaved. 'The bread of mourners will be theirs'. Since it is eaten in a pagan land and in a place of mourning, it will spread defilement, as does anything which is in contact with death.

The bread they eat will have nothing to do with meals in honour of Yahweh. 'Their bread will be to keep themselves alive', and will have no other purpose. No one will enter the domain – that is, the land – of Yahweh.

⁵What will you do on the day of the festival,
on the day of the feast of Yahweh?

On the day of 'the festival' (the Feast of Tabernacles), they will feel the burden of their being cut off from the worship of Yahweh.

⁶ Surely even if they walk away from destruction,
Egypt will gather them up, Memphis will bury them.
As for their precious idols made of silver –
weeds will acquire them;
thorns will be in their tents.

The prophet envisages the day when the Assyrians arrive. There will be devastation throughout the land. If there are some survivors who escape, and flee in the opposite direction from Assyria, to Egypt, they will find no refuge there. They will die and their bodies will be buried in the burial grounds of Memphis. As they run, their silver idols will be abandoned, and weeds will overgrow the places where the idols were abandoned. The tents that were used as shrines for the idols will be deserted and thorns will grow up in them.

The people will lose the privilege of worshipping Yahweh in the way he wanted. Whereas once they had indulged in pagan worship, when Israel will be overtaken by the invading forces, in their distress they will want to worship Yahweh, but they will not be able to do so. Where they are going, there will be no wine-offering symbolising dedication to God, no bread symbolising that God is their life and sustenance. Their old idols will let them down but, by the time they realise it, it will no longer be possible for them to turn back to the system of worship in the law. The land will be lost and Yahweh will no longer be able to be worshipped in the way he had required.

3. *Without him, God's people lose their insight.*

When the prophet announces that 'The days of retribution have arrived', the people's only response is ridicule: 'the prophet is a fool'.

> [7] The days of punishment have come,
> the days of retribution have arrived;
> let Israel know it!
> 'The prophet is a fool,
> 'the man of the Spirit is crazy!'

Hosea parodies what the people say about him and others like him. Quotation marks bring out the sense.

The next line is part of the prophet's reply. His announcement of retribution may be thought insane, but the prophet knows otherwise.

> No, it is because of the greatness of your iniquity,
> it is because your hostility is great.

Then he goes on to explain the role of a prophet.

> [8] With God, the prophet is a watchman over Ephraim.

The presence of a prophet in Israel is a great privilege. He is like a watchman. He is like the watchman in 2 Samuel 13:34 who, in the days of Absalom's rebellion, saw first the approach of David's other sons, and sent his information to the king as an early report of what was happening. It is like the incident in 2 Samuel 18:24-27, where the watchman observes before anyone else the approach of a messenger (see also 1 Samuel 14:16; the imagery is developed in Ezekiel 33:1-6).

The prophet is a 'watchman' in that he knows God's will before others. He gets advance knowledge. Also, the prophet is a person who has the courage to announce what he knows so that others get warning. It is this that is likely to bring the slander. 'The prophet is a fool', people will say, for not everyone will believe him.

'With God' refers to the fact that the prophet gets his knowledge by 'standing in the counsel of Yahweh' (see 1 Kings 22:19; Jeremiah 23:22; Amos 3:7).

The prophet is likely to be the object of many plots. Hosea refers to the nation when he says

The snare of a bird catcher is in all his ways,
and there is only hostility in the domain of his God.
⁹ They have gone deep in depravity,
as in the days of Gibeah.
He will remember their iniquity;
he will punish their sins.

The 'house' or 'domain' of God is the land of Israel. Wherever the prophet goes, he meets with opposition to his announcement. But the people 'have gone deep in depravity as in the days of Gibeah'. Hosea refers to the sordid incident in Judges 19-21. The men of Gibeah at that time received inevitable judgement (Judges 20:29-48). Israel's behaviour at this later time and their treatment of Hosea is no better. God will soon punish their sin. When far from God, the people reject the prophetic message, and so they lose their insight into God's will for their lives.

In the church there can be traditionalism without reality. Or habits and customs that have long been in our country get mixed into spiritual life. Then the latest religious philosophy from wealthy and influential countries can get a grip on our thinking. Israel's religion was a mixture of Israelite tradition (the good old ways from the past), Canaanite customs (the pagan habits that had long been in the country) and Assyrian additions (the latest pagan ideas from the most powerful country around). But the result was lost inheritance.

The way forward is the opposite. When God's people lean on him, believe his Word, and trust him despite the pressures that come on them, he gives them an experience of himself as the living God. In him they find an inheritance, they discover true worship, they are given spiritual insight.

Questions for Reflection

1. What is the Christian's inheritance?

2. Is the Christian to be a 'watchmen'?

3. Are pagan customs mixed in with our faith?

21. The Beginning and the End (9:10-17)
The next section in Hosea is a description of the beginning and the end of Israel's story.

1. *The nation had happy beginnings.* Like the beginning of a happy marriage there was close affection between God and Israel at the start.

> ¹⁰ **Israel, I found your forefathers**[42] **to be**
> **like grapes in the wilderness.**

---

42. 'Israel' is addressed by God. The object of the verb is delayed but is the same as in the next line. In English we express the object first.

**I saw them as
the best fruit on the fig tree in its first season.**

Grapes and figs are pictures of sweetness and savour, the 'first-ripe fig' being specially delicious (see Micah 7:1). God's people have a habit of getting things right at the first, and at such a time they are deliciously pleasing to God. If God's people would 'abide' or 'remain' in that happy state, simply developing and enlarging what they have, all would be well (see John 15:4; 1 John 2:24). Israel was for a short time in a happy state of faith, of love, of optimism, knowing that the nation's future was in the hands of God. The 'devotion of your youth', as Jeremiah put it, and 'the love of your betrothals' (Jeremiah 2:2) was specially pleasing to God. The first relationship between Israel, like that between Hosea and Gomer, was a sweet romance. Israel trusted God, and God delighted in them. There were no rivals coming in between them.

It did not require perfection on the part of Israel for the nation to be loved by God. Far from it! When God chose his bride she was in a pitiable state (see Ezekiel 16:6-14). Perfection was not needed, but *responsiveness* was! 'I remember', said God, 'your following after me ... through a land not sown'. Israel's wavering but real eagerness for God showed itself in their following God in the wilderness even before they got to the prosperous land in which they could settle (Jeremiah 2:3). Likewise, the Christian does not have to be sinlessly perfect – he will always need the blood of Christ – but he has to 'walk in the light' and 'hear God's voice'.

2. *Then the nation fell into idolatry.* The 'honeymoon period' of Israel's history came to an end when the nation arrived at Baal-Peor (which is the name of a place as well as the name of a god).

**They came to Baal-Peor and devoted themselves to shame,
and they became as detestable as that which they loved.**

'Baal', the fertility god of the Canaanites, who was thought to supervise wind and rain and clouds, had one particular manifestation as 'Baal-Peor'. He was the god of the mountainous land of the Moabites. When Israel was travelling towards Canaan they had occasion to go through Moab, and they stayed for a while at Shittim, where they 'played the harlot with the daughters of Moab' (Numbers 25:1). This involved a mixture of religion and lasciviousness. They took part in rituals of the pagan cult of Baal-Peor, but one of its attractions was the sexual orgies involved in Canaanite religion. It was the very thing that was prompting God to call for the extermination of the Canaanites! God acted severely. About 24,000 Israelites were killed in a plague (Numbers 25:1-9; Deuteronomy 4:3; Psalm 106:28).

The Christian's 'first love' must keep burning. Paul was referring to precisely this incident at Baal-Peor when he said 'We should not crave evil things ... These things happened to them as an example ...' (see 1 Corinthians 10:1-13). We need to learn to chop down savagely the modern equivalents of Baal. As God's law given through Moses required that the utensils of Baal be cut down (Exodus 23:24) or burned (Deuteronomy 12:3), so the modern forms of Baal – the self-indulgence, the loose and freelance sexuality, the violence, the cult of self-centred money-worshipping – need to be cut down and burnt out of the lives of those who walk in the Holy Spirit.

Otherwise there soon comes a decline. Love for God decays. Enjoyment of his presence takes second place. Prayerlessness becomes habitual. Bitterness towards others creeps into our hearts. There is secret departure from the living God, which eventually becomes public and open. The 'delicious fig' goes sour.

Hosea says 'they became as detestable as that which they loved'. It is a biblical principle that we become like the gods we worship. 'They walked after emptiness and became empty' (Jeremiah 2:5). Equally, fellowship with Jesus produces likeness to Jesus. 'We ... beholding as in a mirror the glory of the Lord ... are being transformed into the same image...' (2 Corinthians 3:18).

It takes only a little bit of flirtation with the idols of the world, and the distinctiveness of God's people is lost.

[11] As for Ephraim, like a bird their glory will fly away.

'Glory' is the radiation of God's character. It might be visible – as it was inside the holy of holies. It might be partially visible, being represented by angels, as it was to Moses (see Exodus 3:2-6; see also Hebrews 1:7). It might be known only by faith (as in 'we beheld his glory' in John 1:14; see also John 2:11). The 'glory' of God in Israel and in the life of the Christian is also the radiance of God's holy character in the life of the nation or in the life of the Christian. He is being changed 'from one level of glory to another' in this world (2 Corinthians 3:18), and his final 'glorification' will be the holiness of his life become visible. In more than one sense 'the glory departs' when God's people sin. In Hosea's day, the nation's distinctiveness would soon be lost, and a century later in Judah the glory would depart from the temple in Jerusalem (Ezekiel 8-11).

3. *Israel's punishment for affirming the idolatry of the nations will be the proven failure of the false gods.* God would bring upon them the very reverse of 'fertility'.

> **There will be no birth, no pregnancy, and no conception!**
> **[12] Though they bring up their children,**
> **yet I will bereave them before the children become adults[43].**
> **Woe to them when I depart from them!**
> **[13] Ephraim, as I have seen, is a fir-tree[44]**
> **planted in a meadow;**
> **but Ephraim has even brought out his children for slaughter.**
> **[14] Give them, O Yahweh – what will you give?**
> **Give them a miscarrying womb and dry breasts.**

Since the gods were revered as the source of fertility, Yahweh will demonstrate that 'there will be no birth' if he withholds fertility. He

---

43. The translation, 'without a person left', is probably incorrect. 'From man' (literal Hebrew) should be taken as a reference to adulthood.
44. The Hebrew word could mean 'to Tyre', but it is also known from late Hebrew as a word for 'fir-tree'.

can actually put the process of fertility into reverse, and take back to himself children already born.

'Woe to them when I depart from them!', says God, implying that until this point he has in some sense been with them. 'She does not know that I gave to her the grain and the wine and the oil' (2:8). Even when Israel was deep in sin, God had been with the nation, without the nation's being aware of it. But if now God actually departs, and they get what they want, God-lessness, they will then realise that they have been experiencing God's provision all along.

The great depths to which Ephraim – that is northern Israel – has sunk is seen in the next lines. The land God gave them was beautiful, but they have even descended to child-sacrifice. In Hebrew, 'slaughter' almost sounds like a name: 'Ephraim has even brought out his children for Slayer'. Whatever the pagans might call their god, Hosea calls it 'Slayer' or 'Murderer'. It is the reverse of fertility!

It is not totally surprising that Hosea prays for justice to be done, asking for 'a miscarrying womb and dry breasts'. He is not speaking in personal vindictiveness. This is still Hosea, the prophet of love! But he knows that this is what is involved in the judgement of God and he is realistic when he prays that God's will may be done. And as a prophet he knows what God's will is. The child-murdering religion of northern Israel must itself be judged and Hosea feels free to pray that it will!

4. *They have despised their greatest blessings and now will lose them.* Gilgal was an old town (Deuteronomy 11:30). It was near Gilgal that the Israelites crossed the river Jordan and it was there that they built a twelve-stone monument commemorating the goodness of God in bringing them to their promised land (Joshua 4:19-24). It was a monument to encourage them always to fear God (Joshua 4:24). In the same area they conducted the first circumcisions in the new land. So Gilgal spoke to them of God's power, and of their pledges of loyalty.

Yet Hosea can say:

> I saw all their evil at Gilgal;
> Indeed, I came to hate them there!
> [15] Because of the wickedness of their deeds
> I will drive them out of my domain!
> I will love them no more; all their princes are rebels.
> [16] Ephraim is stricken, their root is dried up,
> they will bear no fruit.
> Even though they bear children,
> I will slay the precious ones of their womb.

Gilgal, which ought to have spoken of God's power and the new life of his people, actually was the place where kingship began (1 Samuel 11:14-15). Yet their first leader, Saul, was a rebel and in northern Israel the kings have promoted idolatry even in Gilgal. Now the nation will end in invasions, death and deportation. It will be for them the end of an epoch.

> [17] My God will cast them away
> because they have not listened to him;
> and they will be wanderers among the nations.

'If the end of a human action is already contained in its beginning', wrote J.M. Ward, 'what hope is there for a community that makes a bad start?'[45] It depends what the bad start is! The people of Israel made a bad start in wanting a king. God was ready to overlook the matter. It was 'great wickedness' (1 Samuel 12:17) but Samuel said 'Do not fear ... do not turn aside from following the LORD' (1 Samuel 12:20). But a 'bad start' is different when it starts in idolatry and ends in human sacrifice! It is more serious than a faulty and unbelieving decision regarding kingship. Until there is drastic and deep-rooted rejection of idolatry, there is no hope of survival as the people of God. The destined outcome of such a sin is inevitable because God cannot overlook it. It is unforgivable because it was renouncing the means of forgiveness, and unredeemable because it was rejecting the Redeemer.

---

45. See J.M. Ward, *Hosea: A Theological Commentary* (Harper and Row, 1966), p. 155.

Questions for Reflection

1. Is our relationship to God like a 'sweet romance'?

2. What sort of responsiveness does God look for in his bride the church?

3. What hope is there for a community that makes a bad start?

22. Despising the Goodness of God (10:1-8)
Despite all her privileges Israel turned to false gods.

1. First, we consider *the nature of Israel's sin*. Hosea highlights the way in which the nation had shown such ingratitude.

(i) They misused God's gifts (10:1-2).

> **¹ Israel was a luxuriant vine;**
> **it yields fruit for itself.**
> **The more its fruit increased**
> **the more it increased the altars.**
> **The more the land prospered,**
> **the more they adorned sacred stones.**
> **² Their heart is deceitful,**
> **now let them bear their guilt.**
> **He will break down their altars;**
> **he will destroy their sacred stones.**

God brought Israel into a land 'flowing with milk and honey'. God is good to his people and never provides for them in a niggardly way. 'Fertility' is his speciality! He knows how to give life and energy of every kind. The people of Israel were like a luxuriant vine in their prosperity. Quite recently they had had a taste of how prosperous the land could be, for the days of Jeroboam were affluent and easy, although the poor did not get much of a share of the affluence.

But affluence did not result in Israel's gratitude to God. They simply became more self-confident in their idolatrous ways. The more its fruit increased, the more they used their wealth to increase the altars to pagan deities. The more the land prospered, the more they adorned 'sacred stones', upright standing stone pillars erected in honour of a god.

Their sin was misusing God's gifts. When sinners incur no judgement but rather get prosperous it ought to lead them to gratitude. The goodness of God leads us towards repentance (Romans 2:4). But more often than not a hard and impenitent heart is fortified in its godlessness. There is self-deception in this; 'their heart is deceitful'. We deceive ourselves into thinking the goodness of God is indifference. There may be a lengthy time-gap before God acts but the idolater is 'storing up wrath' (Romans 2:5). Soon the implements of idolatry will be broken down.

(ii) They denied God's power (10:2-3).

The people of Israel soon were ignoring their traditional faith in the kingship of God and were ascribing kingship to other gods of Canaan and of Assyria.

> [3] Now they shall say 'We do not acknowledge a King;
> we do not fear Yahweh.
> And the King – what does he do for us?'

From earliest days Israel had been gripped with the conviction that God was a king. The arrangement of the camp of Israel in the wilderness was like that of an army with the tabernacle as the royal pavilion at its centre. The ark within the tabernacle was God's throne. Samuel regarded the demand for a king as wicked because 'Yahweh your God was your king' (1 Samuel 12:12). Now the vision of God's kingship has so faded that they are not acknowledging Yahweh as king at all. Again, their view of God is that of a prosperity cult; 'what does he do for us?' is their only question. Evidently they felt Baal might do better than Yahweh and it was to the pagan god that they were giving the title 'king'. They no longer viewed Yahweh as having power over their enemies, or over the forces of nature, or over the destiny of the nations.

In the words 'We do not acknowledge a king' the parallel line shows that God is the king concerned. The people valued human kingship, both that of Israel and that of Assyria, but they virtually renounced the kingship of Yahweh. When the people of God are in serious decline they doubt God's power. They forget their own history in which God has acted powerfully, and they begin to look to other entities as the source of strength and the hope for deliverance.

(iii) They deserted God's covenant (10:4).
Hosea refers to 'empty promises'. This seems to refer both to failure to keep oaths made to God, and failure of trustworthiness in conversation generally.

Long ago Israel had made a 'law-covenant' with God, that is, a covenant in which Israel as a junior partner swore oaths of allegiance and obedience to God as senior commander or ruler. A preliminary promise of allegiance had been given on Sinai (see Exodus 19:8), followed by the detailed laws of the covenant (see Exodus 20:1-23:33). Then the oath of obedience was given (Exodus 24:7) and the whole covenant was confirmed by sacrifices in which blood was shed (Exodus 24:8).

But now they were making alliances with Assyria, alliances which would involve treaties in which they called upon the chief god of Assyria.

Lack of seriousness in keeping faith with God led to oath-taking becoming an insincere affair altogether. All kinds of oaths and solemn contracts then became casual matters.

⁴ **They make promises,**
taking empty oaths,
making covenants.
So lawsuits spring up like poisonous weeds,
in the furrows of the field.

The covenants with Assyria would be exactly analogous to the one they had with Yahweh. The Israelites would be involved in pagan sacrifices and pagan rites. They were in effect repudiating their covenant with God and making alliances with fake deities.

One illustration of 'empty oaths' was that taken by Hoshea, Israel's last king. He entered into covenant with the king of Assyria (2 Kings 17:3), but then some time later broke his oaths to Assyria and turned to Egypt instead (2 Kings 17:4). It was a piece of covenant-breaking that was to bring the nation of Israel to an end.

Meanwhile the result of casual oath-taking was that society became riddled with endless lawsuits. Lawsuits sprang up 'like poisonous weeds, in the furrows of the field'. As Calvin pointed out[46], one expects poisonous weeds in the countryside but not in well-ploughed fields. Israel had been well prepared by God, but turning away from God's covenant left the poisonous weeds of abounding social injustice in Israel, the very field where God had done so much.

2. Secondly, we consider *the consequent judgement of God.* The people will learn that they have 'stored up' wrath but that now there is to be a 'Day of wrath' (Romans 2:4-5).

(i) They will experience God's deprivation (10:5-6a). God will take away their idol altogether.

> [5] **They fear for the calf-idols of Beth-Aven,**
> **and for the one who dwells[47] in Samaria.**
> **His people will mourn over him,**
> **his idol-priests will grieve over him,**

---

46. J. Calvin, *Commentaries on the Twelve Minor Prophets*, vol. 1 (Banner of Truth reprint, 1986), p. 358.

47. Despite many translations, 'one who dwells' cannot easily be the subject of a plural verb. In Numbers 35:34 the verbal root is used of Yahweh ('I Yahweh dwell...'); here it seems to be used of a false god. This is confirmed by the way the sentence goes on to speak of 'he' – the false god.

> those who rejoiced over its splendour.
> For he has departed into exile from them.
> **⁶Also, he will be carried to Assyria as a gift to the great king.**[48]

Hosea fixes his attention on two northern towns. The first was Bethel, nicked-named Beth-Aven, 'House of Wickedness', found in 10:8 in a short form, 'Aven'. Bethel, or 'Aven' – Wickedness – was known for its idolatrous sanctuary in which gods were represented by statues of calves, representing God or the gods. The other town was Samaria in which there was one particular deity. Hosea calls it 'the Resident'. God was meant to 'dwell' or 'reside' among his people (Numbers 35:34) but Samaria's 'Resident' was an idol. Evidently in the capital city there was one particular god whom the people revered. Soon he will be carried off by the Assyrians. His people will mourn over him. The professional priests who have made a living out of idolatrous religion will grieve. The idol was evidently quite gorgeous to look at. There were people who 'rejoiced over its splendour', but the god will be exiled just as will the people. He will become a novelty in the collection of the king of Assyria, an antique for his friends to admire.

(ii) They will face shame and fear (10:6b-8).
When God's day of judgement comes there is exposure and everything is seen for what it really is. One result is shame.

> **Ephraim will receive shame;**
> **Israel will be ashamed of its image.**
> **⁷Samaria's king will be cut off**
> **like a twig of wood on the surface of the water.**
> **⁸And the high places of Aven – the sin of Israel –**
> **will be destroyed.**
> **Thorns and thistles will grow up**
> **on their altars;**
> **and they shall cry to the mountains 'Cover us!'**
> **and to the hills 'Fall on us!'**

---

48. As before (see Hosea 5:13) *mlk yrb* should be read as *mlky rb*, ('the great king').

In God's judgement the worthlessness of all of our idols becomes plain and obvious. The image that Samaria had once taken such pride in (10:5) will now become an object of shame and disgrace. It will have no more permanence or significance than a chip of wood floating away on a stream of water. 'High places' will be destroyed so as to be no more than a pile of rubbish. The people who worshipped the idols will have such fear that the very mountains and hills will be invited to bury them out of sight and away from the appearance of God's wrath.

Exposure, shame, insignificance, destruction, fear – these are all characteristics of the New Testament teaching concerning hell. What happened in Israel at a purely mundane level within earthly history will one day happen at an eternal level and will never be reversed.

God's judgement involves exposure. There is nothing secret that shall not be disclosed (see Luke 8:17; 12:2).

God's judgement involves shame. Jesus endured the cross despising the shame. In hell, men and women will endure the shame, having despised the cross. Men and women shrink in shame at his coming (1 John 2:28).

God's judgement involves lost significance. Men and women become without destiny, significance or purpose. Israel's experience foreshadows the eternal experience of the wicked. Hell is a place of loneliness, of being ignored. Hell is exclusion (2 Thessalonians 1:9). It is Jesus saying 'Depart from me' (Matthew 7:23; 25:41; Luke 13:27). It is being outside the banquet-hall, outside the wedding feast, outside the shut door. The lost want access to Jesus but are excluded (Luke 13:25). They are thrust out (Luke 13:28). They are isolated from God's people and go to 'outer darkness', and for ever are no more than 'a twig of wood on the surface of the water'.

God's judgement involves destruction, ruination (Matthew 7:13; Romans 9:22; Philippians 1:28; 3:19; 2 Thessalonians 2:3; 1 Timothy 6:19; Hebrews 10:39; 2 Peter 2:1, 3; 3:7, 16; Revelation 17:8,11).

God's judgement involves fear. Hosea's words are echoed by

Revelation which indicates that what men and women would say in 723 BC, will be echoed at the appearing of Jesus. 'They called to the mountains and the rocks, "Fall on us and hide us from the face of him who sits on the throne, and from the wrath of the lamb"' (Revelation 6:16).

Questions for Reflection

1. Does the modern Christian ever have to take an oath?

2. Should a Christian fear judgment?

3. How much should a Christian be preoccupied with what God can do for us?

23. Seeking the Lord (10:9-15)

The thread of argument in this section goes through six steps. (i) Israel has persisted in sin since the days of Gibeah (10:9a); (ii) war is God's way of chastening (10:9b); (iii) Israel had great potential for serving God, since God had provided sufficient resources for national righteousness (10:10-11); (iv) even now Hosea calls the nation to seek God (10:12); (v) but Israel has sowed bad seed (10:13) and (vi) total destruction is near at hand (10:14-15).

We may express this in six principles.

1. *God acts in judgement only slowly* (10:9a). Hosea mentions an event at Gibeah which had happened about four centuries before his time.

**Since the days of Gibeah you have sinned, O Israel,
and there you have remained.**

The story is as follows. A Levite and his concubine had quarrelled. The girl went back home, and the Levite went to Judah to get her back. As they were travelling, late at night, they arrived at Gibeah, a town just north of Jerusalem which at that time was inhabited by Jebusites. In Gibeah, an elderly man gave the couple hospitality, but while they were at his home, the obscene and vile men of Gibeah wanted to homosexually abuse the visiting stranger. So sordid was the culture of the day, two girls were offered instead, and the townsmen abused the Levite's slave-wife so violently that by the morning she was seriously injured and soon died. The Levite from Ephraim went home with the body, dismembered the corpse and sent pieces to twelve districts of the land (Judges 19:1-29).

It led to civil war. The tribe of Benjamin was almost annihilated (Judges 20:1-46).

Now it is four centuries later, but Gibeah's perversity is still typical of the nation. The references in Hosea to Gibeah (5:8; 9:9; 10:9) suggest that the town was still a centre of sin.

Hosea maintains that northern Israel has not changed! Still the nation is in total moral chaos and everyone is doing what is right in his own eyes. The people of Israel, like the men of Gibeah, are still immoral, violent, uncompassionate, murderous, hideously cruel, and prone to civil war.

God is about to judge the nation, but no one can complain that it has been given no time. Far from it! They had had at least four hundred years – but it had produced no change. God gives plenty of time. The question is: how do we use the time he gives us? Since the days of Gibeah Israel had persisted in the same habits. 'There you have remained' is Hosea's way of saying that the life-style of Israel had not changed.

2. *God allows the violence of society to be its own punishment* (10:9b-10). In the days of Gibeah, the nation regretted its extreme measures in almost exterminating the tribe of Benjamin (to which Gibeah belonged). They had sworn not to give any girl in marriage to any Benjaminite. Then they called a meeting at which they were wondering how to provide wives for the survivors. Then they discovered that the men of Jabesh Gilead had not come to the meeting (Judges 21:1-9). So having almost wiped out Benjamin they now

felt they should wipe out Jabesh Gilead also! Things are not so
different in Hosea's time.

> Truly the battle in Gibeah will overflow them,
> because of the sons of wickedness.
> ¹⁰ In my determination, I chastised them,
> and the peoples shall gather against them
> when I punish them for their double iniquity.

In the days of the judges the battle against the Benjaminites went so
far that they almost exterminated the tribe; in this sense it 'over-
flowed them'. It was caused by the 'sons of wickedness' in Gibeah,
the Benjaminite town. The other people of Israel gathered against
Benjamin. God himself gave his permission to them. All this is
paralleled still in Hosea's time. 'There they have remained'.

The situation is the same. Violence is overflowing in Israel, so
they will be given more of it. Do the nations want violence? They
will get it – in civil war, resembling the time of the incident at
Gibeah, and in Assyrian invasion.

3. *When God saves his people he gives them sufficient resources
to live for him.* The people of God have sufficient grace to live
lives of righteousness (10:11).

> ¹¹ And Ephraim – whom I love –
> is a heifer, trained to thresh the grain.
> I have put a yoke upon her fair neck.[49]
> I harnessed Ephraim; Judah may cultivate the ground.
> Let Jacob break up the ground for himself.

The picture language here all speaks of the great potential that there
was in Israel. The nation was like a well-trained cow or ox, ready
for working on the farmland. The different parts of Ephraim and
Judah were all well-trained under the yoke of God's training. Ephraim

---

49. The Hebrew *'brty* should be pointed as a pi'el; and *'l* is the Hebrew
word 'yoke'.

in the north and Judah in the south, were equally prepared by God for serving him. 'Jacob', the whole nation, was well equipped. One remembers that in Israel the farmers were forbidden to muzzle the ox (Deuteronomy 25:4), so the ox was abundantly provided for. God gave the nation status as his people. He promised his protection. He gave them his law. He furnished them with a system of worship, and regulations that would keep them distinct from the surrounding nations. They had promises to look forward to. They were 'a heifer, trained ... harnessed', enabled by God himself to serve him.

4. *God shows great mercy, in inviting us to return to him, despite much sin* (10:12). Even at this late stage in the story, Hosea invites the nation to come back and reverse the trend of what was happening in the land. The agricultural picture-language continues. He speaks of sowing seed, of reaping a harvest, and of breaking up ground. Also the thought of God's sending rain is still agricultural language. What would be the good of breaking up ground and sowing seed, if there were no rain.

> [12]Sow for yourself the seed of righteousness.
> Reap the harvest of mercy.
> Break up your hard ground.
> Surely it is time to seek Yahweh,
> until he comes and showers righteousness upon you.

He puts to them a principle of sowing and reaping. If they want a change in the life of Israel there is something they must do. God has provided everything that they needed. God was ready to give them help. He had given them guidance and put them under a yoke of his discipline. He was ready to bring them into a life of righteousness. But it would take involvement on their part.

If they would 'sow a seed' of righteousness, God would be ready to show them a harvest of mercy. This means that God would show mercy towards them, but also it means that if they would return to righteousness, the people of Israel would become a

people of mercy, rather than, like the men of Gibeah, a society of
merciless savagery.

He tells them that they must firmly take themselves in hand.
They had been in wickedness and hardness for many years. They
were like hard soil, but they need to break up the hardness of the
ground. It would mean facing what they had become and resolving
to look to God to break habits that had become entrenched in their
national life.

He calls them to seek God ('Surely it is time to seek Yahweh'),
and, on behalf of God, tells them what will happen if they do ('...until
he comes and showers righteousness upon you'). To seek God
means to find out what his will is, to follow after the experience of
his presence as the living God. If they will live in such a way, God
will pour out on them the experiences and rewards of righteousness.

5. *God calls upon us to face seriously the sins we have been engaged in* (10:13). Hosea still uses agricultural imagery when he
challenges the people to face what the nation has actually been
doing.

> ¹³ **You have planted wickedness,**
> **you have reaped iniquity,**
> **you have eaten the fruit of lies.**
> **For you trusted in your own way,**
> **and in the multitude of your warriors.**

Sowing and reaping is a principle that will apply to other kinds of
seed than the seed of righteousness. Wickedness had been a seed
sown in the life of the nation for many years; now they were reaping the consequences in the chaotically wicked life of Israel. The
root of the whole lifestyle was self-trust.

Verses 12 and 13 make a striking contrast. Instead of sowing
righteousness (10:12) they have planted wickedness. Instead of
mercy (10:12) there was iniquity. Instead of gaining showers of
righteousness they were reaping habits of ever more entrenched
iniquity. But at the root was a deeper matter. Instead of seeking

Yahweh (10:12) they were trusting themselves, both their habits ('your own way') and their own political and military power ('the multitude of your warriors').

6. *God gives final warning: destruction is near at hand* (10:14-15). God's mercy shows itself in his warnings. God would not be giving warnings at all if there were not a possibility of restoration.

> [14] **A tumult shall arise among your people,**
> **and all your fortresses will be destroyed,**
> **as Shalman spoiled Beth-Arbel in the day of battle.**
> **Mothers were dashed in pieces beside their sons.**
> [15] **So will he do to you, at Bethel,**
> **because of your great wickedness.**
> **At dawn, the king of Israel**
> **shall be completely ruined.**

A tumult – the chaos brought by invading armies – will arise among the people of Israel. 'Shalman' is apparently an abbreviation for Shalmanesar and refers to the invasion of Israel by Shalmanesar I in the early days of Jehu's reign, in which a town called Beth-Arbel was apparently treated with great severity.[50] At dawn – at an early stage of the battle – the king will be defeated thoroughly and easily.

God gives final warnings. In Israel's case it happened as Hosea had said. Another Shalmanesar – the fifth – invaded Israel. Hoshea the king was captured and lost his kingship for ever (2 Kings 17:4).

There is really no choice to 'sowing the seed of righteousness'. The only alternative to the showers of righteousness is complete ruination. A day of reckoning faces us all sooner or later. The alternative that faces us all is between the breaking up of hard ground so that we find God's showers of righteousness or the imminent and irreversible collapse of all hopes and the annihilation of all our joys as the ways of sin bring their results.

---

50. Other possibilities are Shalmanesar V (but the date of Hosea 10:13 is probably not so late) or Shalmanu the Moabite king (but he is a more obscure figure).

Questions for Reflection

1. Is sin its own punishment?

2. What are the Christian 'sufficient resources'?

3. How do we break up 'hard ground'?

24. Called from Egypt (11:1-4)

Sin is ingratitude. It is rejection of love. It is a thankless lack of response to God's initiative in showing great mercy.

1. *God shows great love in setting his heart upon his people.* God's treatment of Israel at the time of the nation's youth brought into being a sweet and happy relationship at first (see 9:10; 10:1; 13:1, 4-6).

> ¹ **When Israel was a youngster I loved him,**
> **and I called my son out of Egypt.**

God showed *unconditional love*. 'I loved him' refers to God's setting his heart upon the nation of Israel. There was no reason for it, within Israel itself. 'The LORD loved you ... because the LORD loved you' is all that can be said (see Deuteronomy 7:7, 8). It is simply a matter of God's 'purpose and grace' (see 2 Timothy 1:9). Israel was idolatrous, wretched, in no way different from other nations in sinfulness, when God placed his love upon the nation.

God *chose Israel for sonship*. God made the entire nation his son. It involved God's concern, and his planning the future for his youngster, the nation of Israel. He trained him as a father teaches skills to his son. He guided the youngster in the way he should go. At the cost of all the firstborn sons of Egypt, God redeemed his Son (Exodus 11:5).

God *allowed hardship in the nation's life*. Although God set his love upon the nation, God seemed to neglect his son, and allowed suffering in his life. For a long time his beloved son was allowed to remain in Egypt in distress and in bondage.

But eventually God *called the nation into privileges of liberty and maturity.* To 'call' in this setting is not merely to invite, but to powerfully summon. God 'made bare his mighty arm' and powerfully drew Israel out of the land of bondage. Nine miraculous judgements took place (Exodus 7:14-10:29) yet the nation could not escape. The tenth miracle was a battle over firstborn sons. God judged the firstborn sons of the Egyptians but redeemed his own firstborn son by the blood of the lamb (Exodus 11:1-12:50). Before the blood was shed the nation could not get out of Egypt; once the blood had been shed the nation could no longer stay in. God powerfully 'summoned' his Son out of Egypt, saving the nation by the blood of the lamb.

Matthew's Gospel (2:15) applies Hosea 11:1 to Jesus. These experiences in the story of Israel are repeated in the story of Jesus. Of course, Matthew 2:15 is not a quotation of a direct *prediction* of Jesus' departure from Egypt. Sceptics are missing the point when they accuse Matthew of a misquotation. Hosea 11:1 does not *predict* anything explicit about the Messiah, and Calvin rightly said long ago that only 'those not well versed in Scripture' apply it directly to Christ.[51] Matthew is not crudely twisting Hosea; he is *expounding* Hosea 11:1 and *re-applying* its principle.

God has a habit of (i) sovereignly setting his love on people, then (ii) bringing them into the status of being his sons, and then (iii) despite his love for them, delaying his bringing them into the fullness of what he wants for them. Then (iv) suddenly and surprisingly God brings the chosen ones from bondage to liberty. All of this happened with Israel. All of it happens to Christians; Hosea 11:1 could be applied to them also. We too have, in our own ways, been called out of Egypt (as Revelation 11:8 suggests). God extricates us from bondage, and treats us as his sons. Matthew 2:15 makes the point that what is found in Hosea 11:1 fits Jesus also.

(i) God unconditionally set his love on his Son when he chose him to be the Saviour. Jesus is God's Elect (1 Peter 2:6).

(ii) In more than one way God brought Jesus into sonship.

---

51. Calvin, *Hosea*, p. 386.

Although Jesus was 'son' in sharing the divine nature, he was called
into sonship on earth as the man Jesus Christ. As a human being
Jesus was appointed God's Son to fulfil his Father's will, and so
fulfilled Psalm 2:7, 'You are my Son'.

(iii) Yet, after the Father had brought Jesus into the world as his
Son, there was delay and it seemed impossible that a carpenter's
son would achieve the Father's will. He was poverty-stricken, despised because of the very circumstances of his birth. To escape
the wrath of Herod his parents had to flee to Egypt – of all places!

(iv) But out of Egypt God called his Son! As Israel was drawn
out of obscurity and bondage in Egypt in order to be brought to a
promised land, to be a light to the nations, so Jesus' obscurity and
suffering even as a child came to an end. The Father repeated in
Jesus what he had done for Israel. 'Out of Egypt have I called my
Son' was repeated.

Of course, Matthew knows that he is re-applying Hosea 11:1.
It is not straightforward citation of a prediction. A little meditation
on Matthew's purpose in using Hosea 11:1 in this way reveals how
thoroughly Matthew had grasped the implications of Hosea 11:1. It
is an invitation for us to do the same.

2. *God's call is rivalled by the invitations of the world.* The
Hebrew of verse 2a is simple. 'They called to them', says Hosea.
He has already referred to the daughters of Moab at Baal-Peor
(9:10). At that time 'They called the people to the sacrifices of their
gods' (Numbers 25:2). 'They' (pagan people) called to 'them' (Israel). The sense is 'Others also called to them...'.

> **²Others also called to them;**
> **in this way they departed from me.**[52]
> **They offered sacrifices to Baal,**
> **and to images they burn incense.**

---

52. The Hebrew *mpnyhm* ('from their faces') should be read as two
words, *mpny hm* ('from me ... they').

³ Yet it was I who was a guide[53] for Ephraim,
taking[54] them by the arms.
They did not acknowledge that it was I who healed them.
⁴ I used to pull them with cords of human kindness;
with ties of love.
I was to them like those who take the yoke from off[55] the jaws;
I heard[56] their plea and strengthened[57] them.

There is a conflict of two appeals. There is the powerful calling of God (11:1), but 'Others also' call to us. God's call is a 'high calling', a calling to God's rewards (Philippians 3:14). It is a holy calling (2 Timothy 1:9), a calling of the voice of God from heaven (Hebrews 3:1). It begins as a call into fellowship (1 Corinthians 1:9), and then continues as a calling to holiness (1 Corinthians 1:2). We are to live in a way that is worthy of it (2 Thessalonians 1:11).

But 'Others call also'. God warns us about these 'calls' from elsewhere. 'They will call you to join them', God said to Israel about pagan invitations (Exodus 34:15). But they were rather to hear a call to gratitude. The blessing of Zebulun and Issachar (Deuteronomy 33:18-19) sees the tribe responding with gratitude to God, and says 'They will call the people to the mountain' for worship of God.

---

53. The traditional rendering, 'I taught Ephraim to walk', is mistaken. A youngster (*na`ar*) does not need to be taught to walk, and Ephraim is not the object of the verb. The unusual verb form means 'to lead, to walk ahead'. See Andersen and Freedman, *Hosea*, p. 579.

54. Translations that have 'I took' presuppose an emended text. If we leave the MT as it is, the word could be an imperative or an infinitive absolute. I suggest it is the latter, and that it is used with the sense of 'taking them' (compare the infinitive absolute in Numbers 15:35 – 'the whole assembly stoning them').

55. With a verb containing the idea of 'motion-away' the Hebrew preposition may mean 'from off '.

56. The verb is well attested with the meaning 'to incline', to 'heed'.

57. The verb is *ykl*, to 'enable' or 'be able'. There is no connection with *'kl*, 'to eat' or (in its hiphil) 'to feed'.

So there are two kinds of call. Israel heard the appealing beguilements and invitations of paganism nearby. Listening to the blandishments of the girls of Moab, they were drawn into pagan immorality and, as part-and-parcel of pagan life, into pagan religion.

Hosea sees this as deep ingratitude. They had experienced God's guidance ('I ... was a guide...'), which had been very detailed and personal; God had 'taken them by the arms' in showing them the precise way in which they should follow him.

They knew quite clearly that they had been extricated from bondage in Egypt and had been given privileges of free rescue. He had miraculously delivered them from Pharaoh who sought to get them back and bring them into his possession once again. God had firmly put down Pharaoh's attempts to regain the people, and had slowly and gently taken them by a route which did not put too much pressure on them and gave them time to recover from their experiences in Egypt. 'God did not lead them on the road through the Philistine country ... God said, They might think they will have to fight' (Exodus 13:17, NCV). By his gentle methods he gave them complete recovery from the hardships they had endured for so long. Yet, despite all this, 'They did not acknowledge that it was I who healed them'.

His discipline was gentle and humane. He promised to keep his covenant 'for a thousand lifetimes' (Deuteronomy 7:9). He was like a father coaxing and gently persuading an adolescent inclined to go his own way, not pushing him with brutal tyranny but pulling him with cords of human kindness, using ties of love, looking for gratitude and responsiveness.

He brought to an end all of the suffering of the Israelites in Egypt, and was to them 'like those who take the yoke from off the jaws'. Lifting a yoke was a symbol of liberation (see Genesis 27:40). God had heard their plea. When they had groaned because of the heaviness of their burdens (Exodus 2:23), God had been taking notice. 'I heard their plea and strengthened them', says God.

There are many ways of looking at sin. God wants us to see it not simply as becoming vulnerable to punishment, or as setting ourselves up for disgrace – although those also are ways of looking at sin. Yet the highest way to view sin is to see it as ingratitude. God has done so much for us. When we are sinning against him, we are not sinning against a policeman, government, or headmaster. To sin against the God who has saved us is ingratitude. It is sinning against a husband, against a rescuer, against the world's greatest Lover. Hosea knew what it felt like. Sin is not simply to be a criminal, a transgressor. It is to be a cad, a louse, an imbecile, a nincompoop, treating the love of God with scorn. If we see it that way we shall fall on our knees and ask for forgiveness.

Questions for Reflection

1. Is love ever really unconditional?

2. Is Matthew 2:15 a fair use of Hosea?

3. What is the best way to get ourselves to hate sin?

25. Loved with Everlasting Love (11:5-11)

Israel's sin is deep ingratitude. They have heartlessly brushed aside God's goodness to them (11:1-4). Now Hosea says that they will face disaster because of what they have done.

1. *They will experience what it is to 'return to Egypt'.* 'He' in verse 5 still refers to 'God's youngster', Israel.

> [5] He shall surely[58] return to the land of Egypt,
> and Assyria will be his king,
> for they have refused to turn around.
> [6] The sword shall whirl against their cities,
> and it will finish off his sorcerers,

---

58. The Massoretic *l'* should be read as an asseverative lamed, 'surely'; in verse 11 the people are envisaged as going to Egypt.

and consume them in their plots.
⁷ My people are determined to turn from me,
and to their 'High God' they call,
but their god cannot lift them up at all.[59]

Hosea predicts that they will return to Egypt. Some see here a
negative statement: 'He shall not return into the land of Egypt'[60].
More probably, the Hebrew text means they will 'surely' return to
Egypt. They will return to the *experience* of what it was like in
Egypt, when they get deported by the Assyrians. Once again they
will groan in bondage (see Exodus 2:23). They will face exile (11:5)
and military devastation (11:6). Their 'sorcerers' ('oracle-priests'
or diviners in Israel's corrupt religion) will be killed. In the middle
of their political intrigues the sorcerers will come to an end at the
time of military invasion.

2. *Their persistence in sin gives God a problem.* Israel has ada-
mantly refused to repent (11:5). Its political life no longer has any
contact with Yahweh but is steered by the schemes of the religious
leaders. The nation's religious life is now dominated by Baal, their
'High God'. They call to him, but when the invasion comes as it
soon will their god will be of no help.

So they will experience what it is to 'return to Egypt'. It is as
though they will be 'un-redeemed'. It is this ghastly thought that
confronts God. He is in agony and deeply pained at the thought of
losing his people. He cannot be reconciled to the idea of losing
them at all.

---

59. The subject of the sentence is literally 'he'; the *hw* at the end of 7b is
to be taken as the subject of line 7c. In translation it is best to repeat 'their
god'. *Yachad* means 'entirely' or (with a negative) 'at all'. See D.A.
Hubbard, *Hosea: An Introduction and Commentary*, IVP, 1989, p. 192,
n.2).
60. See A. Cohen, *The Twelve Prophets* (Soncino, 1948), p. 43. 'Soncino'
commentaries keep close to the MT.

> [8] How can I give you up, O Ephraim?
> How can I hand you over, O Israel?
> How can I make you like Admah?
> How can I treat you like Zeboiim?
> My heart is turned over within me;
> my emotions are aroused together.
> [9] I will not execute the burning of my anger,
> I will not turn around to destroy Ephraim,
> for I am God and not man,
> I am the Holy One among you,
> and I will not come in anger.

The fiercest conceivable wrath is about to fall on the nation. God is heart-broken at their disloyalty. Hosea was a deeply affectionate man, the kind of husband who is constantly showering affection on the one he loves. It tore him to pieces when he could get no like response from Gomer. But, as he discovered, God feels the same way. Only heart-rendingly painful experiences give us a shadow of how God feels when his people show no response of obedience and communicativeness. Sinfulness in God's people is a problem even to God himself! He cannot bring himself to reverse their redemption in reality – though he may put them through an experience which is comparable to their becoming unredeemed. So God says 'How can I give you up ... hand you over ...? How can I make you like Admah ... like Zeboiim?' Admah and Zeboiim were cities which in company with Sodom and Gomorrah were totally destroyed and annihilated in the destruction by fire and sulphur, as told in Genesis 19. Since the coast of the Dead Sea has changed position, their remains are now under water at its southern end. God asks: can I finish altogether with Israel? He cannot bring himself to take such a step.

The idea that God is 'without passions' (as was the Greek philosophers' idea of God) is quite misleading. God says 'My heart is turned over within me; my emotions are aroused together'. Aristotle's god was an 'unmoved mover'. He was immune to pain, unchangeable, without pathos or involvement in history. The God of the bible is altogether different.

3. *God is committed to his people no matter what they do!* There could be no greater statement threatening loss of status as God's people than to speak of being taken back to where they had been before they were redeemed by the blood of the lamb. It is a threat of 'un-redemption', yet covenant-blood sanctifies for ever, and God cannot bring himself to take such a step.

> ⁹ I will not execute the burning of my anger,
> I will not turn around to destroy Ephraim,
> for I am God and not man,
> I am the Holy One among you,
> and I will not come in anger.

The words, 'I am God and not man' (11:9), are associated with oath-taking. It was when God solemnly affirmed to Saul that his kingship was lost that he used similar language (1 Samuel 15:29). It was in connection with the unshakable security of the nation of Israel that similar language was used by Balaam: 'God is not a human being, that he should lie, not a mortal that he should change his mind'. Of course the Bible *does* portray God as 'changing his mind', but not after an oath has been taken! When such a solemn affirmation as a covenant-oath is given, change is impossible. 'Did he ever say something and not do it? Did he ever promise something and not make it stand?' (Numbers 23:19). Before the oath, the promises could possibly be lost, and before the oath threats can be averted by repentance. But even God is irrevocably committed once the oath is given.

The 'difficulty' for God consisted in the fact that he had sworn to Abraham that his seed would endure. God's people can be 'unredeemed' in their *experience,* although they are not *literally* un-redeemed. Israel did not *actually* go back to Egypt. Yet in being taken to Assyria they were experiencing again what they had experienced in Egypt before their redemption.

No matter how much God gives his people the *experience* of being un-redeemed, it never comes to the total reverse of redemption in objective reality because God has taken an oath! Similarly, the high-priestly work of Jesus on behalf of his elect cannot cease because God has 'sworn for ever and will not change his mind'. The unqualified and unconditional promise to David could not cease because an oath had been taken. If David's sons forsake God's law, there can be remedial punishment, but God says 'I will not break off my lovingkindness ... My covenant will I not violate, nor will I alter the utterance of my lips' (Psalm 89:30-34). The key sentence in Psalm 89 is the next one: 'I have sworn ...' (verse 35). Once an oath is taken God cannot change his mind.

The same principle applied to northern Israel. Just as in the south God had given an oath to David, so in the north God's people were covered and protected by the oath that had been given to Abraham.

It is because God is 'God and not man' in the matter of oath-taking that Israel cannot be set aside, no matter what the nation might do, no matter how low it might sink.

It is significant that God goes on to say 'I am the Holy One among you'. When God takes an oath, he swears 'by his holiness'. He cannot back out of an oath without ceasing to be holy. It is 'impossible for God to lie' (Hebrews 6:18) because God resolves to stay as he is – the holy God. God swears that he will continue to be God! When God's truthfulness, God's holiness and God's utterly secure oath-taking are all taken into account, it produces what the letter to the Hebrews calls 'an end of every dispute ... the unchangeableness of his purpose ... strong encouragement ... an anchor of the soul'.

God's elect nation, Israel, could not be finally lost. The nation still exists today, and God still has plans for it. Similarly for the Christian, all the 'oaths' of God that he will protect Abraham's seed apply to him or her. Psalm 89:30 can be reapplied: if God's sons fail to walk in the Holy Spirit he will visit their transgressions with the rod, but he will not break off his lovingkindness to them.

There was powerful wrath operating against northern Israel, in the eighth century BC. In one sense it ceased to exist – so severe was the disciplinary wrath of God. Yet 2 Chronicles 30:11 and 30:18-20 reveal that remnants of the northern territory took refuge with the south, and this increased during the days of Josiah (2 Chronicles 34:6-7, 9; 35:18). The area known as 'Samaria' continued and it was still sacred to God. The gospel would specially be taken to 'Samaria' eventually. God did not execute the burning of his anger so severely that he destroyed Israel for ever. Yet the events were severe enough! There was 'eternal security' for Israel, yet it worked out along a pathway of great suffering.

4. *Despite all Israel's sin, God's purpose will be fulfilled.* Hosea's final word in this section is optimistic.

> ¹⁰**They shall walk after Yahweh,**
> **like a lion he will roar.**
> **For he will roar and his sons will come trembling from the west.**
> ¹¹**They will come trembling like birds from Egypt,**
> **and like doves from the land of Assyria,**
> **and I will settle them in their houses – oracle of Yahweh.**

Eventually they will follow Yahweh, who will be like a roaring lion amidst the nations. His roars are his acting in judgement through international events, acting in such a way as to enable the return of Israel.

Israel's spiritual restoration – with masses of Gentiles incorporated into it – will be like a bird returning to its nest. The restored ones would have a new eagerness to sin no more, and would in that sense 'come trembling', and would come back to provision and protection in a new land. God would settle them in the land of promise once again.

This would take place in a tiny way when northern Israelites would come to Jerusalem in later years. It would take place in a yet greater way when Samaritans would turn to the Saviour who died and rose again in Jerusalem. In Romans 11:12, 15, 26-29 Paul indicates that there is yet more to come.

Questions for Reflection

1. Can we return to the experience of being unsaved?

2. Does God really have a problem with sin?

3. Can God change his mind?

26. Jacob the Deceiver (11:12-12:5)

Hosea points next to the deeply ingrained deceit in the life of Israel. Verses 1-13 of chapter 12 belong together. On the other hand we shall see that verse 14 has more links with the following section than with this one.

1. First, Hosea puts to us *the national deceitfulness of Israel* (11:12-12:2).

> **¹²Ephraim has surrounded me with deceit;**
> **the house of Israel has surrounded me with treachery.**
> **Judah also is a rebel[61] against God,**
> **against the faithful Holy One.**
> **¹ Ephraim is striving after wind,**
> **and follows after the east wind.**
> **They multiply falsehood and violence;**
> **they make covenant with Assyria**
> **and take oil to Egypt.**
> **² Yahweh has a lawsuit against Israel,**
> **to punish Jacob according to his ways,**
> **according to his deeds he will punish him.**

Yahweh is the speaker. He laments the deceitfulness of the entire nation ('Ephraim ... Israel ... Judah'). Both Israel and Judah are pretending to be loyal to God but in fact are deep in idolatry (11:12).

---

61. The meaning of *rad* is uncertain. 'Rebel' fits and it is possible there is a verbal root, *rdy*, 'to renounce' (see Genesis 27:40). Another possibility is 'vagabond'.

They are trying to attain the unattainable ('striving after wind') in seeking national prosperity and stability while disregarding Yahweh. The Mosaic law had long before predicted nothing but war, ravages and famine for Israel if they would not heed his law. Yet they were becoming increasingly deceitful in their betrayal of Yahweh, increasingly violent in their society and political life, and they were getting involved in covenants with Assyria that involved acknowledging their gods. 'Taking oil to Egypt' is apparently a reference to covenants made with oil, a practice that was not known in Israel but was followed elsewhere (12:1).

This deceit, violence and treachery will only bring havoc upon Israel. They are in covenant with Yahweh; God still demands that they submit to the requirements he laid upon the entire nation at the time of the covenant-making upon mount Sinai. God will hold a lawsuit, a prosecution in which he calls Israel to account (12:2), and then issues sentence.

2. Next, the mention of Jacob and his 'ways' and 'deeds' (11:11) recalls the story of the ancestor of the nation, Jacob, and leads Hosea to point to some *lessons from the life of Jacob the deceiver* (12:3-5). The ingrained deceitfulness of Israel is nothing new. The forefather of the nation – Jacob who was renamed Israel – was a man of ingrained and habitual deceitfulness. The people of Israel are 'Jacob' indeed – just like their ancestor. And yet there are other lessons to be learned from the story of Jacob. He was a deceiver and yet experienced God's grace. The nation of Israel centuries later would do well to meditate on his entire life.

> [3] In the womb he seized his brother,
> in his manhood he struggled with God.
> [4] He struggled with an angel and he prevailed;
> he wept and begged for God's favour.
> At Bethel God found him,
> there he spoke to him,
> [5] Yahweh, the God who is omnipotent,
> Yahweh is his name ever to be remembered.

The description of Jacob is not in chronological order. It picks out what happened at his birth (3a), then jumps to an incident that took place at Peniel (3b-4b), and then goes back to what had happened at Bethel (4c-4d). The three incidents point to three things Israel needs to recall.

(i) *He was chosen despite weakness of character* (12:3a). 'In the womb he seized his brother...'. Deceptiveness and grasping ways were characteristic of Jacob all his life. He was born grasping his brother's heel, and went on being a grabber and deceiver all his life. He tricked Esau out of his birthright, and then tricked his father Isaac into confirming by testamentary oath what had happened between him and Esau. The posture in which he was born turned out to be prophetic of his life and his character.

And yet he was chosen by God. God determined to use him. Before he had done anything good or bad God declared what his purpose was for Jacob. The nation of Israel would come from him.

The nation of Israel needed to remember this in Hosea's day – and still does in ours. Jacob was chosen by grace, God was determined to make a nation out of him and use that nation to bring blessing to the world.

(ii) *The greatest events of his life came when he became desperate to get God's help* (12:3b). We recall the story. Because of his bad relationship Jacob had to run away from home. God met him at Bethel. He went on to stay with his uncle, Laban, in Aram. Twenty years later he returned home. But as he was returning home the news came that Esau, the one whom he had deeply offended years before, was coming to meet him. Jacob had tried to escape from Esau because he feared Esau's threats of murder. Jacob was desperate. He came to Peniel by the river Jabbok. On one side was Jacob; on the other side, coming to meet him, was Esau. Jacob believed his life was in danger.

Then God appeared to him. An angel, representing God, appeared to Jacob in the visible and palpable form of a human being. It is possible to say 'Jacob met God' or 'Jacob met an angel' or 'Jacob met a man'. All three are valid ways of speaking.

Jacob 'struggled with an angel and he prevailed; he wept and begged for God's favour'. This was the greatest moment of Jacob's life. He was determined to get help and was holding on to God for dear life (12:4a). 'I will not let you go unless you bless me', he said.

He was emotional. He wept (12:4b). God takes notice of our need. It is not that we force ourselves to weep, but when our state is such that we are weeping, he is moved by our need.

Jacob humbled himself; he 'begged for God's favour' (12:4b). Hosea points to these incidents in the life of Jacob because it was what the later 'Israel' needed. Jacob prevailed with God and received God's blessing by determination to lay hold of God and get his request answered. Yet the Israel of Hosea's day is characterised by unconcern and prayerlessness. Jacob humbled himself and as a result became 'Israel' – a prince with God. But now the Israel of Hosea's day is full of pride and is getting nothing from God. Soon Assyria will wipe it out of existence altogether.

The Israel of Hosea's time had Jacob's grasping character, but when would they be like him and grasp hold of God, with Jacob's intensity, emotion and entreaty?

(iii) *The starting point was in God's grace* (12:4d-5). Hosea moves back a stage to an earlier event. 'At Bethel God found him; there he spoke to him'.

The hope for the nation of Israel was the grace of God. Hosea's reminiscences jump back to an earlier point in Jacob's life, because the event at Peniel was not the start of God's relationship with Jacob. There had been an encounter even earlier at Bethel. At that time, when Jacob was desperate and was in distress and suffering, God simply stepped into his life. Jacob had done nothing to seek God at all. His story was simply one of deceit. He had brought bad trouble upon himself. But while he was running away God met him. Jacob took no step towards God; God took a step towards him. 'God is in this place and I did not know it' was Jacob's reaction.

God was then a God of grace, and – Hosea is suggesting – God is still the same. The point is underlined by the names that Hosea uses. God is 'Yahweh, the God who is omnipotent; Yahweh is his name ever to be remembered'.

Two names point to the power and graciousness of God. God is 'Lord Almighty' or 'the Lord who is omnipotent' – Lord Sabaoth as we have it in Romans 9:29 and James 5:4. The phrase strictly means 'Lord who *is* hosts'. The Hebrew does not have a 'construct-genitive' ('of hosts') but has two nouns in apposition ('God who *is* hosts'). The idea is not that God is lord 'of' something (armies? stars and planets? bits and pieces of creation?) but leads us to think of God as full of unbounded powers and resources. He has within himself 'hosts' of potentialities and assets, capacities and energies, which give him the wherewithal to meet every situation with effortless ease. 'Lord Almighty' is the translation that grasps the heart of the matter.

Also God is 'Yahweh', the God who redeems by the blood of the lamb. When Moses was summoned to be the mediator of a new phase of God's salvation he asked the question 'What does your name mean?'. The reply was given 'I am who I am', or later in the same verse, simply 'I am' (Exodus 3:14). The name 'Yahweh' is clearly related to this revelation of the divine name. Although the linguistics of the matter are complicated, the main point is clear and indisputable. 'Yahweh' is short-hand for 'I am that I am'. God revealed what he is in the events of the Exodus. The name refers to *events*, not to anything metaphysical (such as immutability or self-existence). 'Look at what I am about to do', says God in effect. 'Look at me in action; I am about to get myself a name' (Nehemiah 9:10). The name 'I am that I am' refers to history. It is not what God is in himself. It is not a prediction, but it refers to what God will show himself to be. 'When you see me in action', said God, 'you see what I am. What I am about to show myself as being in these coming events – that is what I am.' Who then is the God who gave himself the name 'Yahweh'? To put it simply we can say 'Yahweh' means the God of the Exodus, the God who takes a people for himself and who redeems them by the blood of a lamb. This is the inner essence of the character of God and it is by this memorial-name that he is ever to be remembered.

This is what God had showed himself to be in Israel's history. He had taken the twister, Jacob, and turned him into a 'prince with God'. He had taken a community of enslaved suffering descendants of Jacob in pagan Egypt and had rescued them by the blood of a lamb. Hosea points them to their own history. Let the nation believe in the God of Jacob. Let the nation believe in the God who rescues by grace. And then (see 12:6) let them turn back to their God.

Questions for Reflection

1. Does God really choose people?

2. Is God affected by tears?

3. Does God have a personal name?

27. A Rescue on Offer (12:6-13)
Hosea has referred to the national deceitfulness of Israel (11:12-12:2), and compared it to the life of Jacob (12:3-5). Now he continues to draw out some further implications. Throughout the section he is making the point that rescue is on offer. Jacob was born with a somewhat twisted personality. He was born with a grasping disposition. Yet God rescued him and he is today among the heroes of faith. What was possible for Jacob himself is possible also for his descendants. God does not change and therefore the sons of Jacob are not consumed (Malachi 3:6).

1. *Repentance will bring recovery* (12:6).
Jacob found blessing from God when he learned, in his desperation, to wait on God. Now, says Hosea, let the nation do the same.

> **⁶ But you, with the help of your God, must return.**
> **Observe mercy and justice,**
> **and wait constantly on your God.**

Instead of trying to find purpose and success in life through deceit, Israel is invited to find recovery in repentance, that is, in a return to mercy and kindness. The word here is *chesedh*; we have seen it before (4:1; 6:4, 6; 10:12). It is love, kindness, mercy, mutual loyalty.

Israel must find recovery in 'justice'. The word here is *mishpat* which means 'good judgement', 'righteous decision', national conformity to God's will and God's ways.

Israel must find recovery in a new determination to seek and find God's will. They must 'wait constantly on your God'. The verb refers to a particular kind of praying. In other contexts it means to lie in wait (e.g. Psalm 119:95) or to expect something (Isaiah 64:3). In contexts of prayer it refers to the kind of praying where the answer does not come immediately but one has to 'wait' on the Lord. The psalmist said 'On you I wait all the day' (Psalm 25:5) and prayed 'Preserve me, for I wait on you' (Psalm 25:21). It refers to the kind of combination of living-and-praying which is focused on the hope that God will hear our prayers and reward our faith.

It is noticeable that Hosea describes here what 'returning' will involve. It is a real amendment of national life, a reintroduction of the values of mercy and justice into the vitality of the country. It is this style of living which would bring recovery to the nation.

2. *Deceit withholds blessing* (12:7-8).

Israel was far from wanting to 'wait on' God. In the 8th century BC the nation was following not the devotedness of Jacob but his deceit.

> **⁷Canaan has false scales in his hand.**
> **He loves to exploit people.**

Dishonesty in business was the fashion of the day. Hosea was offering them a way back to God, but their interest was far more in the successes that pagan religion would bring to their business.

The 'Canaanites' were the original inhabitants of the land. Israel was told to exterminate them, so vile were their habits and morals. After Joshua's conquest they were confined to the coastal region and became famous for travelling far and wide in order to do business. The word 'Canaanite' virtually meant 'trader' (see Proverbs 31:24; Job 40:30; Zephaniah 1:11; Ezekiel 17:4). But now it is the Israelites who are being called 'Canaanites'! Their religion is more like that of the original Canaanite than like the faith given to them by God. Their interest in pagan ways is self-centred and has more to do with getting rich than with pleasing God.

So the typical up-and-coming Israelite stands in the market-place with crooked scales in his hands, and boasts of how well he is doing in life. Baal has blessed him! Yet his religion is idolatrous and only serves in the exploitation of people. Yet he has no shame about his corruption.

> [8] Ephraim says, 'Yes, I am rich;
> I have found wealth for myself'.

In a society where money is everything, success is measured only by business-successes. The corrupt businessman feels no guilt about the methods he is using, although he feels the need to protest his innocence.

> In all my gains they will not find in me
> any crookedness that can be called sin.

Actually they are protesting too much! The reason they feel the need to deny any sinfulness is because they are conscious of it but will not allow themselves to face the wickedness of their ways.

3. *Sinning against redemption is especially grievous* (12:9-12).
The constant theme of Hosea's prophecy is that the sin of Israel is sin against love, sin against God's redemption.

> **⁹But I am Yahweh your God**
> **because of what happened in the land of Egypt.**
> **Once more I will make you dwell in tents**
> **as in the days of the festival.**

It is one thing for a Canaanite to be a Canaanite; it is another thing for the people of Israel to become like Canaanites. God takes seriously his ownership of his people. Israel may have become a Canaanite but Yahweh is still Yahweh! Israel is sinning against the God who had redeemed him by the blood of the lamb. It is a serious matter to sin against one's redemption. Only the people of God can sin in this way, 'profaning the blood of the covenant' (Hebrews 10:29).

What will God do? He will put them through some of the processes of redemption again. It is not that the blood can be shed again. If we sin wilfully there is no other blood that can be shed. The redeeming blood can only be shed once! So God does not take them back to Egypt and have the lamb die for their redemption again.

But he can take them back to the wilderness! Their 'Canaanite' way of life must end. They will lose the privilege of residence in houses and will go back to living in tents, just as they do when they keep the Festival of Tabernacles.

Verse 10 continues the theme of sinning against redemption. They sinned against prophecy.

> ¹⁰ **I spoke to the prophets,**
> **and I sent many a vision;**
> **and told parables through them.**

It was a high privilege for Israel to have prophets sent to them. No other nation received communications from God in this way. The prophets had received messages from God in a variety of ways. Sometimes it was a matter of enlightened and quickened understanding. Sometimes it was a revelation being directly given to the prophet's heart and mind. Many times they received visions, visual representations of what God was wanting to say to his people. We have no 'visions' reported by Hosea, although his contemporary Amos received them (see Amos 7:1-9; 8:1-3; 9:1-4 for five of them). Often the prophets spoke in similitudes, and of these we have an abundance in Hosea's prophecy.

4. *Deceivers can be rescued* (12:11-13).
Verse 11 makes the point that such sinning against redemption brings worthlessness and uselessness.

> **¹¹ If Gilead is evil,
> how futile they have become!
> They sacrifice bulls in Gilgal.
> Yes, their altars will be like a pile of rubble
> in a ploughed field.**

Clearly Gilead and Gilgal were centres of idolatry. Yet all that their religion has achieved is to bring worthlessness and uselessness into their lives. The pagan altars will soon be nothing but heaps of stones. Deceit brings worthlessness; in the long run nothing is achieved by it. It is the lesson of Jacob's life again.

> **¹² Jacob fled to the country of Aram;
> Israel worked to get a wife,
> and to pay for her he looked after sheep.**

Jacob was chosen by God. At the time of his birth, his mother Rebekah, felt that something unusual was happening within her, and asked God for an explanation of it. She was given an answer: two nations would come from the twins who were about to be born. Israel would be senior to Esau in the purposes of God (Genesis 25:22-23). Jacob had not yet been born. He had done nothing good or bad, but without any reference to his character, God made a choice about using him in his future plan. Paul uses the story to teach God's sovereignty (Romans 9:10-13).

As time went on, it became clear that Jacob had a grasping

character. He was born grasping his brother's heel (Genesis 25:26) and the event was prophetic. He manipulated his brother into taking an oath giving away his inheritance rights (Genesis 25:28-34) and similarly tricked Isaac into giving Jacob, not Esau, the headship of the family (Genesis 27:1-27). It brought disaster into Jacob's life and he had little choice but to run for his life.

When Jacob was running away from home because of the deceitfulness that had brought threats of violence against himself, what disgrace it brought! He had to run away in humiliation and dishonour ('Jacob fled ...'); it led to fourteen years of arduous and difficult work for a hard-hearted uncle ('Israel worked to get a wife'); despite the great oracle that had come to his mother at the time of his birth he was working to pay off a debt ('to pay for her ...') and there was little sign of any great future ('... he looked after sheep').

The deceit of Jacob brought nothing but disgrace and delay in God's purpose. The Israel of Hosea's time is tacitly invited to learn a lesson. God has chosen the nation. He is not planning to abandon his purpose, but as originally there was nothing but disgrace, and delay of Israel's usefulness for Jacob when he approached life with deceit, so the nation too will face disgrace, toil, and degradation while it continues in deceitful ways.

So the section ends with a reminder of what happened. Jacob's life was a tough one. Streaks of his old self-protectiveness stayed with him all his life, but God worked through him nevertheless. His people were taken to Egypt. There, all of the promises that had been given to Jacob were fulfilled in the redemption from Egypt. The crucial factor was 'a prophet', Moses. Jacob was 'predestined'; God was determined to use him. But his lifelong deceit only brought suffering. Even his loss of Joseph for many years stemmed from his foolish favouritism. But Jacob, the fugitive, the deceiver, was chosen by God and nothing made that choice fall aside.

Yet the crucial forward step in the story of the people of Jacob came when God sent them a prophet.

> ¹³ **Yahweh used a prophet to bring Israel up from Egypt,**
> **by a prophet he cared for him**.

Yes, the deceiver can turn out well! Hosea gives them a hint; they
are hearing a prophet now – Hosea himself. The descendants of
crafty Jacob had been rescued by a prophet before. They are still
'deceitful Jacob' but let Hosea's words sink in, and let them be
rescued by a prophet again. God is still the 'God of Jacob'. He still
has an unshakable plan for Israel, but for that plan to come to
realisation, repentance and submission to God is required.

Questions for Reflection

1. How should we measure success?

2. If we sin against grace what happens?

3. How often can we ask God for explanations of strange events?

28. The Lion, the Leopard and the Bear (12:14-13:11)
Hosea 12:14 belongs with 13:1-16. Hosea 12:14 and 13:1 belong
together. Ephraim sinned by bringing about death; so God spoke
concerning Ephraim and brought about Ephraim's death. And both
12:14 and 13:1 belong with 13:2-16 where the reversal of death will
be one of its themes (13:14). The chapter has small, well-defined
units.

1. *Murder invites God's capital punishment* (12:14-13:1). We saw
that much of Hosea 11:12-12:13 held together around the theme
of Jacob's proclivity for deception. Now Hosea 12:14 starts a section where the theme is not deceit but violence.

> ¹⁴**Ephraim has provoked God to anger, causing bitterness;**
> **and God will leave the guilt of bloodshed on him;**
> **and his Lord will bring back his reproach on him.**

[1] **Truly he spoke to Ephraim terrifyingly,**
he lifted up his voice against Israel.
He became guilty at Baal, and died.

Murder is a crime which has some unique aspects to it. It cannot be treated lightly. More than many sins it arouses God's extreme vexation. A society which has become so violent that murder is treated lightly is in the terminal stages of decadence. Blood that is shed in violence 'cries from the ground' (Genesis 4:10). Under the Mosaic law there was no atonement for murder. It was a capital crime, and itself required execution. Today, it is alarming how, via television, toy guns, and computer games, our children are schooled from their earliest days to consider killing a light and easy thing. The move from fantasy to reality must surely not be difficult. Yet from the earliest days of world history there has been something so sacred about man's being created as the image of God that murder is in a category all of its own.

Hosea traces the murderous society of his day back to the idolatry which began at Baal Peor (see 9:10). Baal Peor was the definitive occasion when Israel showed its eagerness for idolatry and with it came the seeds of murder and social decay of every kind. With regard to such matters God 'spoke to Ephraim terrifyingly'. Even before the events of Baal Peor God's voice had come amidst thunders and terrors condemning murder and idolatry with excruciating sternness.

At Baal, Israel died. It is not that the nation ceased to exist immediately. 'Death' is a process in Hebrew thinking. But a definitive decision in favour of idolatry was taken there which unless radically repudiated would destroy the nation. It never was repudiated. It was restrained during the days of David but surfaced again after David's death.

2. *Idolatry brings about extermination* (13:2-3). Israel never repudiated its idolatry at Baal Peor. Rather they confirmed it and added to it.

² Now they sin more and more,
and make images for themselves,
idols made from silver by their own skill.
Those who sacrifice human beings speak to the idols[62];
they kiss the bulls.

The idolatry which began at Baal Peor got worse, once the reign of
David was over. The people made images. Soon the Baalism had
become so vile that human sacrifice was being practised. We have
evidence that human sacrifice came into the false religion of Israel
at the low points of its history. Manasseh who sacrificed his son (2
Kings 21:6) is the most well-known example, and there are various
places in Hosea's prophecy which seem to allude to human sacrifice. Some of them are debateable[63], but this verse is scarcely to be
disputed. In plain, simple Hebrew the text speaks of 'those who
sacrifice men'. So much for 'fertility'! The religion which was supposed to promote life actually engaged in ritual killings! At such a
time the idol received a ritualistic kiss (see 1 Kings 19:18, where the
reference to kissing is literal).

But idolatry is self-destructive.

³ So they will be like the morning cloud,
and like dew which soon disappears,
like chaff which is blown away from the threshing floor,
and like smoke from a chimney.

Hosea uses four pictures for extermination: morning cloud, dew,
chaff and smoke. All four are entities which disappear. Idolatry is
inherently destructive.

3. *God is offended when we forget his past mercies* (13:4-6). The
tragedy of Israel was that its sin was sin against all that God had

---

62. The Hebrew says 'them' but it is the idols who are in mind, not the
sacrificed human beings.
63. See Andersen, *Hosea*, pp. 338-339, 631-632, 649.

done for them. Hosea puts before them God's redemption and care
(13:4, 5) in contrast to Israel's forgetfulness (13:6).

> **⁴Yet I, Yahweh, have been your God,**
> **ever since what happened in the land of Egypt.**
> **And you were not to know any God except me,**
> **for there is no Saviour except me.**
> **⁵I cared for you in the wilderness,**
> **in the land of drought.**
> **⁶When I fed them they became self-satisfied,**
> **and because they were satisfied their heart became proud.**
> **Therefore they forgot me.**

God reminds them of his name. God is ever to be remembered as
'Yahweh', the God who gave his name significance when he redeemed his people by the blood of a lamb.

God reminds them of their redemption, specifically recalling
Egypt. Can they not remember from their own history, the bondage
they had been in, and their cries to God? Can they not remember
how he had stepped into their lives and within a short time had
rescued them from oppression? Have they forgotten the wonders,
the dramatic interventions when Pharaoh was wanting to hold on
to them?

God reminds them of his requirement. After saving them he
put before them his requirement that they should have no other
gods before him. He alone had saved them. He alone had brought
them out of the tyranny they had been experiencing. Why should
they turn to the gods of the nations which had proved themselves
weak and fallible and unable to give help in time of trouble?

God reminds them of his uniqueness. 'There is no Saviour except me'. Had any other god, any other philosophy, any other pro-
gramme of action, rescued them in this way? God is Saviour. He
rescues us from the guilt and the pollution and even – partially now,
totally in the end – from all the consequences of sin. Can any one
else or anything else do the same?

God reminds them of his faithfulness to them. 'I cared for you

in the wilderness, in the land of drought'. He had not saved them,
only to leave them to fend for themselves. His initial rescue had
been followed up by wonder after wonder. Manna had fallen from
heaven; water had gushed out for them in the desert. Every need
had been met. Even when they sinned he still carried them on ea-
gle's wings. How can they sin against such a God?

God's very goodness to them was the occasion of their fall.
'When I fed them they became self-satisfied'. When God is good
to us we have a habit of attributing what he does to luck or mere
good fortune. Israel was well-fed and came into a land flowing with
milk and honey. But before a short time had gone by they were no
longer attributing their good fortune to God. It was taken for granted,
as if they had deserved it and as if it had simply come to them
because they were a worthy cause! God's very goodness to us has
a danger attached. We can take it for granted or misinterpret it. The
goodness of God is designed to lead us into gratitude and responsiveness to God in the way we live! It is a symptom of human
wickedness that it can have the opposite effect.

First came satisfaction, then came pride. Last came forgetfulness. Eventually all that God had done became a distant memory;
Israel ceased to recall that they had been redeemed by blood and
then taken to Sinai to worship God and receive his requirements.

4. *God's chastening anger is finally ferocious* (13:7-8). God is
slow to act. He does not deal with us as our sins deserve. Yet when
he does act, it is a fearful thing to fall into his hands.

> [7] **So I will become like a lion to them,**
> **like a leopard I will wait by the roadside.**
> [8] **I will attack them like a bear robbed of her cubs;**
> **I will rip open their insides.**
> **Then I will devour them like a lioness,**
> **like wild animals that tear them apart.**

One must remember a passage such as this when one thinks of
Hosea 'the prophet of love'. While there is amazing compassion in

God and he says 'How can I give you up?' in a voice of great distress, yet this does not mean that he is a weak lover standing by hoping for better days.

His love sometimes requires that he express his wrath. What we have here is *chastising love*, the determination of God to use whatever is needed to bring his people back to him. If he has to be a lion, a leopard, a bear, then he is willing that it should be that way.

He prefers to deal with his people by his Word, but if he is unsuccessful with his Word he can 'attack' them with his hand in the way he rules the world.

5. *Amidst God's wrath God's people are helpless* (13:9-11). The essential nature of Israel, its self-centredness and self-reliance, is now exposed as useless and destructive.

> 9 **It has destroyed you, Israel,**
> **because you are against me, against your helper.**
> 10 **Where now is your king? Where?**
> **and your deliverer in all your cities?**
> **and your judges about whom you said,**
> **Give me a king and princes.**
> 11 **I gave you a king in my anger;**
> **and I took him away in my wrath.**

Their disregard for the help of God has destroyed them (13:9). Years previously they had demanded a king having become dissatisfied with the kingship of Yahweh. God answered them and allowed them to experiment with kingship for more than three centuries. Now it is possible to ask what the result has been. The truth is that human kingship has destroyed them. God was, in his anger, giving them what they wanted when he gave Saul as king to their ancestors. Now God is taking the kingship away. After the fall of Samaria and, a century later, the fall of Jerusalem, that kind of kingship will never be allowed again.

Kingship led to the domination of man-made ideas. The end result has been a society full of murder and idolatry, and a society programmed for self-destruction. They have forgotten what it was like to live dependent on God alone. They have only aroused God's anger. The supposed advantages of living in dependence upon human deliverers never materialised. Now they are helpless. There is only one thing they can do, and that is to throw themselves on God's mercy and live directly under his kingship once again. They will then re-experience his grace.

Questions for Reflection

1. Is the crime of murder to be always regarded as demanding the death sentence?

2. Is God really ever ferocious?

3. What can we do to re-experience God's grace?

29. The Defeat of Sheol (13:12-16)
There have been points in the prophecy thus far where Hosea has virtually predicted the death of the nation, yet at the same time there have been descriptions of a glorious future. Their number will be as the sand of the sea (1:10); they will become God's people again (1:10). They will seek him (5:15); they will be revived (6:2).

Hosea has left these different pictures of the future somewhat in tension. Questions are left in the reader's mind. Has Israel lost its status as God's people? Has Israel 'died' never to be seen on earth again? How can it be that Israel will ever experience such blessing again, if it is to 'die' and disappear as the chaff is blown away from the threshing floor (13:3)?

Hosea is now approaching a resolution of the difficulty. The wages of sin is indeed death, but God is a God of resurrection!

1. *Every sin is kept on record until decision is made concerning it.* In the normal run of events sin cannot be simply forgotten.

**¹² The iniquity of Ephraim is bound up;
his sin is kept in store.**

Sin leaves a permanent record in the mind of God. Hosea's metaphor builds on the Mosaic law; Deuteronomy 32:34-35 spoke of a
locked store in which the sins of a 'nation lacking in counsel' (verse
28) are kept. Vengeance belongs to God, said the Song of Moses
(verse 35), and in due time, not very far ahead, God's judgement
would fall. The judgements would involve life and death. 'It is I
who put to death and give life' (verse 39).

God delays his judgement. It is stored up because it does not
take immediate effect. Yet the fact that judgement is delayed does
not mean that the sin has been forgotten. At any point it might be
brought out to face assessment and recompense.

2. *Israel is foolish in not taking the opportunity being given* (13:13).
The position of Israel is like childbirth, considered not from the
viewpoint of the woman but from the viewpoint of the child.

**The pains of childbirth come upon him;
he is not a wise son;
it is a time when he should not be delaying
at the occasion for birth.**

A child is about to be born. Yet the child is not a wise child and
delays in being born. Of course the picture is not very scientific! It
is simply an illustration. A speedy delivery at the time of birth was
regarded as desirable. Rachel, Jacob's wife, went through protracted
and severe labour in which she lost her life (Genesis 35:16-19).

The idea is that the nation is being offered an opportunity of
new birth, and it will be foolish indeed if it does not cooperate in
getting born. It is a picture of obstinate senselessness in refusing to
change when an opportunity is being given. The child lingers at the
thought of being born, even though the mother's birth pangs put
pressure on the child. It is an unusual picture, but Hosea more than
any other biblical writer knows how to use striking similitudes.

Israel is experiencing agonizing pangs as the Assyrians get ever nearer.
Will the nation not see that what is happening to them is constrain-
ing them to come forth in a new kind of life altogether?

3. *Hosea has a long-term vision of the day when death is abolished.* The prophet moves from Israel's present foolishness and
imminent destruction and turns to a long-term hope of the abolition
of death. Hosea has been thinking of death and destruction coming
upon Israel (10:14), and of the time when God lifted up his voice
against Israel and Israel died (13:1). He has referred to the death-
dealing self-destruction of idolatry, in which Israel is exterminated.
Now he turns to the exact opposite: the day when the last enemy,
death, will itself be destroyed.

> **I will ransom them from the power of Sheol;**
> **I will redeem them from death.**

We must reject the line of thought (found in RSV, NEB, and elsewhere) which suggests that the questions are rhetorical questions,
expecting a negative answer. 'Shall I redeem them ...?' In this approach the prophet is envisaged as calling upon Sheol and death to
do their work; God's compassion will not intervene.

There is no hint that there is a question here. There are no
words of interrogation in the Hebrew and nothing that suggests it.
The last section (14:1-9) contains Hosea's greatest appeal for them
to return to God. Are we to think that at this point Yahweh aban-
dons the foolish 'child that refuses to be born', and calls upon death
to do its work? Surely, it would go against everything we know
about Hosea. That is more like the New Testament picture of Satan!

Hosea is envisaging the resurrection of Israel. At various points
he has virtually predicted the death of the nation. God will break
the bow of Israel (1:5) and will not save them (1:6). God has abandoned them (4:17). Their deeds will not permit them to turn to their
God (5:4). Yahweh has withdrawn from them (5:7). They 'died' at
Baal Peor, and have confirmed that death a thousand times over

since that time (13:1). They will be exterminated (13:3) and devoured (13:8). But that is not the whole picture and we know that God cannot give Israel up. What will he do? He will raise Israel from the dead?

The mode of rescue is 'ransoming' of 'redeeming'. The first word (p-d-h) basically means 'to ransom by the payment of a price'. It is associated with rescuing from the death penalty or from bondage. It was used (for example) when an ass was to be sacrificed but its life could be 'ransomed' when a lamb died in its place (Numbers 18:15-17). Or when a slave concubine displeased her owner husband, the law said 'let her be redeemed'; either she or a friend could buy her freedom. In Hosea 13:14 the idea is that as Yahweh put forth his power and used a lamb to deliver Israel from bondage (see 2 Samuel 7:23, Psalm 78:42, and elsewhere), so he will pay whatever price is needed to extricate Israel from the power of Sheol.

The second word used (g-'-l) is similar but has the added idea that the 'redeemer' is related to the redeemed. It is linked with the kinsman-redeemer idea that we know from the book of Ruth, where the kinsman-redeemer had (i) to be able to redeem, (ii) to be entitled to redeem, and (iii) to want to redeem. Boaz met all three requirements and so 'redeemed' Ruth. This word means 'to redeem a relative from distress, bondage or death, by the paying of a price'. It has the idea of a payment or the using of great effort in order to bring about deliverance.

The New Testament develops these ideas when it speaks of Jesus as the 'ransom' for our sins (Matthew 20:28) or as 'redeeming' us by his blood (Romans 3:24; Ephesians 1:7; Hebrews 9:12; 1 Peter 1:18, 19 and elsewhere). Israel is to be rescued by the price-paying of God or by his mighty energy which he 'spends' in order to get Israel. Such a rescue from death is not easy. The problem of sin is so great that it is a problem even to God himself.

In Hosea, as throughout the Bible, the wages of sin is death. It is not simply the physical termination of earthly life. It is ruined relationship with God, and ruined relationships with human beings. It is the state of the human race where brother rises up against brother.

It is the human race in decline. It involves a ruined relationship towards God's creation. The creation that was originally given to him becomes unresponsive. Death involves subjection to physical decay and physical death. Eventually the creative event of Genesis 2:7 will be reversed and men and nations 'go back to the dust' (3:19). Death is removal from the presence of God, a change of location. Sheol is the place-name for death. It is death considered as being a place.

Hosea looks for the nation of Israel to be spiritually 'resurrected' so as to come back to a happy relationship with God where it enjoys the life of God again.

The Bible envisages a restoration of Israel. It was left to the apostle Paul to explain more. He tells us that 'Israel' was primarily a spiritual term for God's true people (Romans 9:6), that God's believing people in the earthly nation of Israel became an ever smaller 'remnant' as time went on (Romans 11:6), that Christian gentiles were grafted into that remnant so that they too became 'Israel' (Romans 11:11-24), and that one day there will be a spiritual awakening in 'national' Israel, and worldwide revival (Romans 11:25-32). Israel gets to be redeemed from Sheol.

One further question demands thought. Was Hosea thinking of individual resurrection from the grave? That is how the pre-Christian Greek Old Testament took it.

It is hard to see how one put any kind of limit to Hosea's prediction. Any *thinking* person would surely have to ask the question, but is Sheol *completely* defeated or is Hosea only speaking of a restoration wholly within this life? Since the 'wages of sin' include physical death as well as damaged relationship to God, *deliverance* from Sheol must mean deliverance from physical death as well as deliverance from a damaged relationship with God.

The triumphant note in Hosea 13:14 confirms the point.

O death, where are your thorns?
O Sheol, where is your sting?

How could Hosea use such triumphant language if he still thought
Sheol would retain dying Israelite believers. Surely his view of the
defeat of death must have been of the highest order for him to be
able to use such a note of triumph.

So Paul had clear vision when he applied Hosea's words to the
resurrection (1 Corinthians 15:55). And he could add a bit more
and tell us what the thorns and the sting actually are. 'The sting of
death is sin' (1 Corinthians 15:56).

4. *Hosea's vision is a long-term one; what is required in the present
is repentance.* He summons Israel to repentance so as to be ready
for the day of deliverance.

> **Compassion will be hidden from my sight.**
> [15] **Though he flourishes among the reeds,**
> **an east wind will come,**
> **the wind of Yahweh will come up from the wilderness.**
> **His fountain will become dry,**
> **and his spring will be dried up.**
> **It will plunder his treasury of every precious thing.**
> [16] **Samaria will be held guilty,**
> **for she has rebelled against her God.**
> **They will fall by the sword,**
> **their little ones will be dashed in pieces,**
> **and their pregnant women will be ripped open.**

Hosea warns that there is no compassion for the moment (13:14,
last line, which belongs with verses 15, 16). Israel will experience
God's drought within its borders (10:15). Ephraim will be like an
orchard blasted by the east wind and being deprived of all its fruit.
And from outside the Assyrians will come (13:16). The long-distance vision of Hosea 14:13 requires that they face God's judgements in the present (13:14a-16) and heed his appeal to return to
him. Only then will they be among the restored 'Israel' who defeat
Sheol.

Questions for Reflection

1. What might it mean for a nation to be spiritually resurrected?

2. Does God pay a price to save us?

3. What does it mean that 'the wages of sin is death'?

30. The Lover's Plea (14:1-9)

For a lot of the time Hosea has portrayed Israel as almost beyond
redemption. Yet he has reasons for hoping for Israel's restoration.
He believes that *eventually* Israel will come back to Yahweh, and
there is always the possibility that some will turn to Yahweh even
now and be an 'Israel within Israel'.

So he presents a final appeal to the nation. Perhaps Hosea the
husband had made a similar appeal to Gomer. One can imagine his
pleas to Gomer. 'You have badly stumbled because of what you
have done. It's alright. I am not angry any more. Come home!'
Hosea the lover had rescued Gomer; Yahweh the Lover wants to
rescue Israel.

1. *Hosea gives an invitation* (14:1-3). There are two Hebrew words
which focus on different aspects of what is generally called
'repentance'. One (*nicham*) means to regret, or feel sorry about
something. The other (*shub*) is used in Hosea 14:1 and means to
'turn' or 'return'. It refers not to feelings but to decisions, to conduct,
to amendment of life.

> ¹ **Return, O Israel, to Yahweh your God,**
> **for you have stumbled because of your iniquity.**

He reinforces his appeal by pointing to what their sins have done to
them. Their sins were not slight mishaps with no lasting effects.
Rather, serious consequences have come to them ('you have stumbled') because of the sins of the nation in which the vast majority
of the population has been involved.

Hosea tells them in detail what to do.

> [2] **Take words with you**
> **and return to Yahweh.**

He emphasizes that they must pray. The precise wording ('Take with you words ...') might seem to be only a lengthy way of saying 'Speak ...'. But the emphatic expression is a way of insisting that they must actually spend time before God with words. A wordless repentance will fail. They must talk! Elsewhere in Hosea he complained that prayerlessness was at the root of much of the sin of Israel. Repeatedly in the life of the nation they had made decisions and had taken action without consulting God. They had acted without speaking any words to God. If now they are to repent they must begin at that point, putting their prayerlessness into reverse and beginning now to actually speak words in God's presence.

The prayer that is needed is a prayer for forgiveness.

> **Say to him, 'Take away all guilt;**
> **accept that which is good,**
> **and we shall offer**
> **the fruit of our lips.**
> [3] **Assyria will not save us;**
> **we shall not ride upon horses;**
> **we shall say no more "Our God"**
> **to the work of our hands.**
> **In you the orphan finds compassion'.**

They ask for his forgiveness and that he should 'accept that which is good', (although the Hebrew could mean 'Accept us, O Good One'). It is not a reference to justification by works but rather refers to what they are about to say. They are about to offer God their worship and they are about to renounce what they have trusted in previously. Before they get to that point they cast themselves on the mercy of God and plead that these good things should be accepted. It is not taken for granted that God will accept them. He could be so angry that he delay his forgiveness.

They tell God that they intend from this time forward to worship him (14:2b). They know that they will be really grateful to experience God's forgiveness in the face of so much accumulated wickedness.

They renounce the very things that they have been putting their trust in for so long. Before, they had been putting their trust in Assyria or in Egypt's powerful military equipment (horses!), a most sophisticated form of contemporary warfare.

They renounce the false religion in which they had put so much hope, and resolve to look to Yahweh alone from this time on.

Their final plea and their only hope was to cast themselves on God's well-known mercy to the orphan. 'In you the orphan finds compassion'. They were far from pleading their good works; they were looking for mercy.

2. *Hosea gives encouraging promises in the name of God* (14:4-8). God draws us with cords of love, winning us to himself with promises of what he will do for us if we turn to him.

He promises that he will heal them.

**⁴ I shall heal their apostasy,
I shall heal them generously
for my anger has turned away from him.**

Years of distance from God will have left scars and habits and signs of damage. But God promises that he will undo it all. They will be abundantly healed. His anger is turned away. There will be nothing in his heart for them except love. No recriminations about their past will rise up to haunt them. It is true for us also. If we come to God through the blood of Jesus, in this way, God will heal our sinful ways. He does it freely, generously. We do not have to 'deserve' it. It is more than forgiveness that he offers. He heals the actual sin itself. He works in our lives so that the power of sin is steadily and increasingly broken. He will remove his chastening anger.

He promises that he will refresh them.

⁵ I shall be like dew to Israel; ...

In the dry seasons of Israel, winds blew in from the Mediterranean Sea and brought heavy dew. It kept the vegetation fresh and green. So the ones who turn to Yahweh will experience the winds of affection blowing in from the sea of God's love, keeping them fresh and virile, steady and strong.

He promises that he will give them fruitfulness and fragrance.

> **⁵ I shall be like dew to Israel;**
> **he will blossom like the lily**
> **and put down his roots like the crocus of Lebanon.**
> **⁶ His branches will spread out**
> **and his beauty will be like the olive tree**
> **and his fragrance like olive of Lebanon.**
> **⁷ They will return and live in its shade,**
> **they will cause the grain to flourish,**
> **they will blossom like the vine.**
> **Its fragrance will be like the vine of Lebanon.**

It is a beautiful picture of poise, spreading influence, strength and freshness. God will give them fruitfulness. There will be fertility in God in more than one sense.

Hosea's closing remarks make the point that this is the only way that such freshness and vigour can come.

> **⁸ O Ephraim, what have I to do with idols?**
> **I have answered him and I looked on him.**
> **I am like a fir-tree with foliage.**
> **It is from me that your fruit is found.**

In an emotional appeal, as ever like an anguished lover, God pleads for the last time. He has no choice in this matter. For one thing God cannot do is cease to be God. 'What have I to do with idols'. God is amazingly slow to judge, amazingly accommodating. Sometimes he is quite scandalously shocking in the people he uses – Jacob, Samson, David, you, me – but there is no way in which he can accommodate himself to idolatry.

He stays with us with amazing faithfulness. He 'answers' us, meeting our needs and many of our quests and questions. He is 'evergreen' towards us, and there is with him no winter of decay. He gives us all we need for life and fruitfulness.

3. *Hosea sums up his message with an appeal for our attention* (14:9). It is not an appeal to everyone but addresses itself only to a limited audience.

> ⁹ **Whoever is wise, let him understand these things.**
> **Whoever is prudent, let him know them.**
> **For the ways of Yahweh are upright,**
> **and righteous people walk in them,**
> **but rebellious people stumble over them.**

It reminds us of the words of Jesus. 'Whoever is wise ... Whoever is prudent ...', says Hosea, anticipating One who says 'He who has ears to hear ...'.

Not everyone is wise. Not everyone has ears to hear. Hosea is aware that some will respond to his teaching, others will not, but the truth about them is that they are not in the state to hear. They are spiritually deaf.

But he asks that those who are wise will become yet wiser by heeding what he has to say. God's enlightenment comes to us one step at a time. We begin by the fear of the LORD which is the beginning of wisdom. But our understanding has to grow and become enlarged in scope.

The reason he gives for our listening is that 'The ways of the LORD are upright, straightforward, aligned with reality'. God's ways correspond to life. They fit the way we are made, and they fit the way in which God has made the world. It is the pathway of righteousness to 'walk in them', to travel through life step-by-step in steady orderly fashion, regularly submitting to what God has taught us and is teaching us. It leads to the joys of a good conscience. It pays off in this life and eternally.

Conversely, 'rebellious people stumble over them'. The highlights of Hosea's message are almost self-evidently convincing to anyone truly wise. His hatred of idolatry, his teaching concerning God's righteousness, God's lordship over history, God's control over life and fertility, and above all God's amazing love and loyalty and compassion – must all appeal to anyone given wisdom from above. To reject his message is a mark of rebellion, a sign of wilful resistance to what our conscience feels is right. The result of such refusal to face reality can only be 'stumbling', a plunge into death and disaster from which there can be no recovery since the way of recovery has already been rejected.

Better to give in to God and let him be the one who pulls us with cords of kindness, with ties of love. Better to know him as the heavenly lover whose heart is turned over in affection for us. Better to run not from him but to him and let there be a Bethel in our lives, where God finds us and speaks to us. The God of Jacob can be our God too, because he does not change and those of us who admit we are 'sons of Jacob' can know that we shall not be consumed, but will be pulled close to him with cords of kindness. We are glad that he has captured us with his passionate affection, and we rejoice in knowing that he holds us with ties of love, saying to us for ever and ever 'How can I give you up?'. He cannot; and so we are safe for ever and can give ourselves to his kingdom and his righteousness.

Questions for Reflection

1. What are the modern equivalents of Assyria's horses?

2. How does sin leave scars?

3. In what way is God like dew?

The following Focus on the Bible Commentaries will be available in 1997.

1 and 2 Chronicles by Richard Pratt
Daniel by Robert Fyall
Hosea by Michael Eaton
Jonah, Micah and Nahum by John L. Mackay
Haggai, Zechariah and Malachi by John L. Mackay
Matthew by Charles Price
Mark by Geoffrey Grogan
Romans by R. C Sproul
2 Corinthians by Geoffrey Grogan
Ephesians by R. C. Sproul
Philippians by Hywel Jones
1 and 2 Thessalonians by David Jackman
1 and 2 Timothy and Titus by Douglas Milne
James by Derek Prime

Christian Focus Publications publish under three imprints.

Mentor contains books of intellectual worth and spiritual value, suitable for all who are concerned at the lack of understanding found in the church today.

Christian Heritage is made up of classics from the past, including writings from the Reformers and the Puritans.

Christian Focus features a wide range of titles, including the Focus on the Bible Commentary Series and the Historymakers biography series. In addition there are books on doctrine, Christian living, and current issues. There are also children's books in this imprint.

All our authors are committed to the inerrancy of Scripture and the uniqueness of Christ.

For details of all Mentor, Christian Heritage, and Christian Focus titles, please write to CFP, Geanies House, Fearn, Ross-shire, IV20 1TW, Great Britain.